"Building on concrete and often vulnerable illustrations from her life and the lives of others in history, Jen Miskov inspires us to trust in and wait on the Lord. The Lord who leads us into storms will also meet us there; He is more than enough and is worth everything."

Craig S. Keener, professor of biblical studies,
Asbury Theological Seminary

"If you're ready to step out of the boat and take risks with Jesus, then you're in the right place. Jen Miskov is one of those people who leads a life of extravagant faith, and in *Walking on Water* she leads you on a journey to do the same."

Jessika Tate, founder, In Faithful Pursuit Ministries

"Jen Miskov is passionately in love with God, and her infectious fervor mixed with her love of history and the Church will awaken passions deep within. I strongly urge you to read this book so that you, too, can gain passion, and experience your call as His beloved."

Theresa Dedmon, creative arts pastor,
Bethel Church Redding

"Jennifer Miskov and I met in an old revival home in Oakland where Frank Bartleman, that great intercessor of Azusa, had prayed one hundred years before. I connected with a woman who carries a revivalist heart burning for the miraculous signs-and-wonders history of the great evangelist women of the past to be manifested today. This book will create faith and stir hunger for the deepest levels of union with God so that you and many others will walk in the kind of miracles that must be demonstrated today in our world. Read it and be transformed."

Lou Engle, cofounder and president, TheCall

"I have known Jen for many years and have witnessed first-hand how her love for Jesus and her love for others has radically impacted and shaped thousands of lives around the world. When I was reading *Walking on Water*, I saw a vision of a wheel with spokes connecting to a hub. I saw each chapter in her book like a spoke on a wheel that was focused on Jesus as the hub that holds everything together. Jen connects each truth with the One who is Truth Himself. I am excited about the way Jen presents the book because each spiritual principle she reveals leads us back to *Jesus*, who is the Source of it all. In *Walking on Water*, you will not only receive great spiritual insight, but also be led to know Him more intimately. I trust and pray that this book will impact your life and inspire you to bring others to know Jesus, influencing many now and also for eternity."

Mel Tari, author, *Like a Mighty Wind*

"When I read Heidi's foreword to *Walking on Water* and then the introduction, I could feel the fire of God. I managed to get through these, and then I simply could not ignore the burning any longer. I slammed my laptop shut and told the two girls sitting in the lounge with me that this book had wrecked me and that I needed to go to my room to worship. I had an overwhelming hunger for Jesus and a desire to be alone with Him and worship Him. It was such a powerful stirring that I simply could not ignore it. I felt a beautiful fresh surrender happen again in that time of worship and throughout the rest of the book, and I knew God was working in my heart and cleaning house. I started reorganizing my schedule and prioritizing chunks of time to be with Him again. I have been taken back to my first love. From that place of intimacy with Him, I now know that I can step out of the boat.

"This book is key in this season and the times we are living in. We are on the cusp of something big, and we need to make sure union and intimacy are our first and main things! *Walking on Water* was truly life changing, and it confirmed what has been in my spirit for a while!"

Sarah Hodgkinson, age 30, Bethel School of Supernatural Ministry first-year student from South Africa

"*Walking on Water* is far more than mere words on a page. It carries a powerful invitation and impartation to become a person of unshakable intimacy and bold faith. The only way to describe my experience reading it was that my heart burned within me. Jen has a special anointing to release hunger through her writing. I found myself wanting to throw down the book and run into my room to be with Jesus, as I felt my spirit being pulled to experience more of God. I love the way Jen writes. She has profound revelation yet expresses it in a way that readers can actually experience for themselves. I am left with a new wave of passion to grow closer to the Lord, having Him truly be my 'one thing,' and a desire to discover what it really means to live a life of courageous faith. I would highly recommend *Walking on Water*."

Kelly Joy Brannan, age 23, Bethel School of Supernatural Ministry second-year student from England

"*Walking on Water* captured my heart to burn for the one thing. When reading this book, I had moments when all I could think to do was get away and be with Jesus; it created an urgency and hunger to be alone with the One I loved. This book is about the miraculous flowing from a place of intimacy; it helped to take away the pressure and the striving and reminded me of the simple truth that it is all about Him. Intimacy births adventure. Jen's book softened my heart and strengthened my courage, and I know it will do the same for you."

Mary Thomason, age 30, Bethel School of Supernatural Ministry second-year student from England

WALKING
on WATER

WALKING
on WATER

Experiencing
a Life of Miracles,
Courageous Faith
and Union with God

JENNIFER A. MISKOV, PH.D.

Chosen
a division of Baker Publishing Group
Minneapolis, Minnesota

Published by Chosen Books
11400 Hampshire Avenue South
Bloomington, Minnesota 55438
www.chosenbooks.com

Chosen Books is a division of
Baker Publishing Group, Grand Rapids, Michigan

Printed in the United States of America

Library of Congress Control Number: 2017941813

ISBN 978-0-8007-9851-2

Cover Design by Brian Bobel

17 18 19 20 21 22 23   7 6 5 4 3 2 1

To my sister, Darla Dake,
who carries fierce determination and courage.
You are one of the most inspiring single mothers I know. The mercy you have experienced and that you demonstrate for others is simply remarkable.

To my brother, Joe Miskov.
You are a true hero, laying down your life to bring relief and refuge for those in the most devastating of circumstances. How you selflessly give your life to love the poor and those who need it the most is truly inspiring.

To Mark Brookes,
a true father to this generation.
You have raised up courageous ones who know what joy is and are marked by the Father's love. Your passion for revival is contagious. Because stadiums await, this book is for you.

To you reading this.
I believe the Lord has destined you to be a burning one who will partner with others to ignite a generation for Jesus. You will burn but will not burn out, because you will keep your eyes on Jesus, remain in Him and surround yourself with family all the days of your life. I pray that you receive this book—a piece of my heart torn out for you—as an offering of love that sparks a fierce determination to take hold of Jesus, no matter what the cost.

Contents

Acknowledgments

I am extremely grateful to Jane Campbell for not giving up on this project or on me. Along with the Holy Spirit, she was a true catalyst for this book. Thanks to all of the team at Chosen for praying into this project and for their hard work to make it a reality. Thanks also to Steve Lawson for being a great agent and for always being willing to champion me.

I am grateful to Sarah Hodgkinson for all of her support and encouragement, as well as each of my intercessors near and far. Special thanks to Heidi and Rolland Baker and the Iris Global family for always believing in me and supporting me through all seasons.

I cannot express my appreciation enough for the Destiny House family for their grace and prayers during my season of writing. I am grateful for the week of prayer and fasting I had with Lindsey Privitera at Destiny House at the end of summer 2016. I felt an increased anointing when I was writing some of the final chapters of this book from our times of saturating in God's presence together. The way Lindsey lives for the one thing and demonstrates the love of Jesus to others is inspiring and moves the heart of God. Nicol Rumstrom has been a faithful friend whose presence is healing and always feels like home to me. Many more saints have been faithful to cover me in prayer and encourage me in this process. The dream of this book would not have been possible without this special family of greats surrounding me in love and support. For this, I am forever grateful.

Foreword

Longing to Be in His Presence

I am thrilled you picked up *Walking on Water*, which was written by one of my awesome spiritual daughters. As you open wide your heart to receive her message, you will be marked by God's great love. You will go on a journey of risking it all to be closer to Jesus. *Walking on Water* is all about slowing down to fix your eyes on Jesus and to remain in Him. Regardless of what has happened in your life up to this point, God in His mercy wants to take you into a deeper place. As you read *Walking on Water*, I pray that God would overtake you and lead you into a greater place of intimacy with Him than you have ever known.

Jesus is so worth our *yes*. He is longing for all of our worship. He wants to take us deeper into His presence. The atmosphere surrounding our lives changes as we give Him all of our worship. Right now, I encourage you to yield your heart to Him; yield your mind, yield your time, yield your spirit and yield your life to God. Let Him come and take you into abandonment in His presence.

If we come into a place of yielded love, then we will come into a place of yielded joy, because we will know who He is. The way we think and act will change. When we yield, the fragrance of Jesus is so strong inside of us that we are propelled by the power of love into a dying world. God wants to take our little lives and breathe in and through them. When we are filled with the glory, we are so yielded and transformed that we believe He is who He says He is, and we bear fruit that brings Him joy.

The things God has done in me as I have yielded to Him are beyond my understanding. He has gone above and beyond what I could ever have imagined. Our movement, Iris Global, continues to grow today because we started slow and stayed low. Lower and slower does not sound right to a world that thinks it is all about higher and faster. But what if we moved lower and slower in listening to the heart of God and the mind of Christ before taking action? We abide in the vine. I encourage you to change the way you use your time. Yield yourself to the One who understands fruitfulness, the One who creates fruit. He is looking for people who will participate and say yes to yielding their hearts to Jesus in total surrender and abandonment. He wants to take you into a place of intimacy, to a place where you are undone.

I had prayed for miracles since I was sixteen years old. I had seen backs, legs and skin problems healed, but I wanted more. At one point in my life I was desperate, wanting more but not knowing how to get it. As I was wooed into His presence and the glory realm became heavier and heavier on me, everything in the miracle realm changed as well. Suddenly, I saw miracles I had never seen before: Paraplegics ran, cancer disappeared, people with deaf ears heard, blind eyes opened and villages of people from other faiths came to Jesus.

I have learned that all miracles, signs and wonders flow from intimacy. We are in a hurry much of the time, but we must slow down to realize that fruitfulness flows from the place of intimacy with Jesus. We can do nothing outside of God, but in Him we can step into the impossible.

More happens in one moment in the anointing than in all of the years of effort and striving. I saw more in one hour in the anointing than in twenty years of striving. It takes only one minute in graced anointing for lives to be completely transformed—only one moment. Whenever I preach, I have just one point—Jesus! Abiding in my Jesus, loving on my Jesus, living my Jesus, just being with my Jesus. Everything that happens flows out of that place. Jesus is calling out from the very depths of His heart, asking us to give Him time. Do you want to give Him the time? Do you want to come into a place where your whole atmosphere shifts into the weighty glory?

After studying theology for ten years at university, I had this idea that lying on the floor and soaking in God's presence for seven days was a bizarre waste of time when there are people out there who are hungry, sick, dying, lost, hurting and unable to get out of their pain. I realized, however, that God incapacitates us at times to change the way we think. If you will allow God to possess you, and if you will give Him the time, then He will give you the resources in the hours you have left to hold the poor, the dying and the broken. You will have the energy of God in you. When you are in Him, then you glorify Him; when you are not, you do not. Being burned out makes Him sad. When you are yielded in His presence and in the heart of God, then you are full of joy.

As the demands on my life increase and I see a greater need to help the poor and pray for healing, I always change my schedule. I take another hour in the prayer closet. I add another hour worshiping. I add another hour in the glory with Jesus in the secret place. I find a way each time it gets busy. Instead of falling into a place of exhaustion, I step into a place of victory and strength. Dwelling in the secret place takes time. If we are in a hurry, we are going to miss it. God wants to change the way we think. We have been pressured by a model of success that causes us to push into things that do not please God. The Lord is saying, *Beloved, if you will come into the glory realm, then things will happen.*

I believe that the busier we become, the more time we need in His presence. I need four to five hours a day in His presence just to function and to face the crowd. I get up early and spend time with Him. When I am losing joy, I find it when I have that time with Him. I also find I am less worried during the day. Some people do not like that I spend that much time soaking, running, walking, swimming in the glory, because they think a lot more could get done if I started my day in meetings earlier. Every cell in my body resists, and I say, *Lord, in the midst of a dying world, I'm going to choose to give You my time. I'm going to give You the most precious offering, the most costly gift that I know how to give—another hour in the secret place. I'm going to give this time with joy. I am going to breathe in the presence of the One I love, and I'm going to give You what You desire most. I'm going to give You a sacrificial offering—a life of worship, a life in Your presence, a life in the glory.*

God wants to open the eyes of your spirit. He wants to show you the secret place. He wants to change the way you think and the way that you use your time. Your time is the most precious gift you could give God. Your time is more valuable than your money, than anything you could lay upon the altar. God is asking you for your time. He wants time with you in the glory, time in the secret place, time in the realm of the spirit, time in the holy glory, time that is abandoned and fully wasted on Him.

I believe God wants to shake each person reading *Walking on Water*. He wants to burn everything that does not bring Him joy. You can produce nothing in yourself, but in God you are unstoppable. Ask for the fire. Let it burn away self-sufficiency, arrogance, pride and the idea that we can do it our way and faster.

Pray this together with me now:

Jesus, I want to be consumed by Your love. Burn in me a fire that will never go out. Set my heart on fire. Make it a burning, blazing torch. Let the glory of Jesus ignite my heart with love. Burn away the chaff, burn away the flesh and burn away the things that don't bring You joy. BURN! Lord, ignite me in this moment. I give myself as a living sacrifice. I give myself as an offering of love. I give myself as a yielded lover. I give You my time. I invite You to change my schedule and to change the way I think. My mind is still too big and my heart too small. Enlarge my heart. Come with Your fire. I yield myself to the fire of Your love. I choose to worship You with my time and with my whole heart.

The heavy glory is falling on some of you reading this right now. Some of you are physically beginning to feel heat. That is God's fire of love marking you. Some of you reading this are going to covenant with God to change your schedule. You are not just reading a book about walking on water and stepping into miracles with great faith. You are soaking in His glorious presence until your misery is turned into joy and your grapes turn into vineyards. You are repositioning your life for greater union with God. You are inviting Him to come and wreck you with His all-consuming love. I ask for the fire of God to fall on each person reading right now. I bless you to be ignited with a fresh fire for intimacy with Jesus as you embark on this journey with the Holy Spirit in *Walking on Water*.

Heidi Baker, Ph.D., founding director, Iris Global

Beginnings

Twenty years ago I never would have imagined that I would be writing a book about walking on water. But this is more than just a book about miracles and doing the impossible; it is an invitation to embark on a journey of learning how to fall more in love. For when we are in love, we will do anything, even the impossible.

Walking on Water is about focus, intimacy and risk. It is about keeping our eyes on Jesus, growing closer to Him and following our yielded hearts at all costs. It is about loving Him for love's sake and about stepping through fear simply to be closer to the One we love. It is about jumping out of the boat to be wherever He is, even if it is in dangerous and unsafe waters.

In Matthew 14:22–33, Peter was led by his heart to walk on water because he wanted to be closer to Jesus. When we want Jesus more than any other lovers, we will do anything to be with Him. When we must have more of Him at all costs, we will not care what people around us will think of our radical acts of love. When we keep our eyes on Him through the storms and continue to draw near to Him in all circumstances, beneath the scenes courageous hope is formed.

Prophetic Vision

In the summer of 2015, I had a vision of being on a boat in the midst of a storm. A captain wearing all yellow was in charge. I felt safe with him there. I also had the sense that Jesus was out in the storm, calling me to be with Him. When I moved toward Him, I became paralyzed with fear. I did not want to leave the security of the boat. I was stuck with one foot in and one foot out, focusing on the "what ifs" and the storm around me. Yet I still felt Jesus was out on the waters, farther into the storm, calling me to Him.

Finally I decided to refocus my gaze on His face. I then gained confidence to pull my other leg around to the outside of the boat and let go. Letting go is usually what happens to us right before a big breakthrough in our lives. I dove into the water and swam to Jesus' feet, where He reached His hands to pull me up. We stood there together for a few moments before He led me to dance on top of the waters. He held my gaze. I could have stayed there for an eternity. Nothing could replace the excitement my heart felt by being with Him in that moment. Everything else faded away in the light of His glory and face.

Like this vision, life is much more exciting when we step out of the boat into perilous waters to do whatever it takes to be closer to Jesus. We can stay safe inside the boat and live mediocre and normal lives and still go to heaven. I wonder, though, what might be awaiting us if we leave our comfort zones and venture out into dangerous waters because Jesus is there. What greater measure of our destinies might be experienced when we recognize Jesus in the midst of the storms and step out to take hold of Him?

Jesus died so that we could live the abundant life here and now (John 10:10). He did not die so that we could live boring, safe and uninspiring lives; nor did He die simply to give us a one-way ticket to heaven. He lived to die so that we could step into the fullness of our destinies and live lives full of adventure, releasing the Kingdom of God wherever we go. This abundant life is filled with healing the sick, casting out demons and raising the dead (Matthew 10:8). But it is also filled with much more, including greater union with Him and fulfillment of the desires of our hearts.

Over the years, I have had the opportunity to step out in faith toward many impossibilities—some successful, others not as much. In the process I have learned to cling to Jesus even more and to get back up when I fall. I have learned that I can never fail because God promises to turn everything around for the good (Romans 8:28). I have experienced what total abandonment feels like. I have put myself in situations in which the deepest parts of my heart have been exposed and laid bare before others. I have felt such raw vulnerability that all I wanted to do was run away and hide. I have experienced what it feels like to be desperate and to have absolutely no other options but God for deliverance. In the midst of some of these extreme acts of surrender, trust and faith, I have seen Him come through and do things beyond what I could ever have dreamed.

Let the Journey Begin

During our journey together in *Walking on Water*, you will discover how falling in love with Jesus is the key to courageous faith to step into the impossible. We will be primarily looking at the story of Peter stepping out of the boat to be with Jesus. You will see this account in a new light, and you will never look at it the same way again. I will share some of my own stories with you and what I have learned along the way. In most chapters of this book, we will also look at the implications for our own lives. You will be challenged with activations that, I believe, will help you live a more free, fearless, passionate, courageous and powerful life of love for Jesus. Do not feel the need to rush through this book. You will get more out of it if you take the time to do the activations as well as process the deeper issues of the heart that arise as you are reading.

I now invite you to join me on this journey into greater intimacy with Jesus with total abandonment. Leave all heavy baggage at home, for you are about to go on the adventure of a lifetime. I believe you will be changed as you embrace this journey wholeheartedly and with full surrender. Do not be afraid—He will give you the strength and courage to step outside the boat to find Him. Jesus is right here, awaiting you with open arms. He is calling you today to meet Him out on the waters.

As you fully yield to the Holy Spirit in this process, I pray that your present reality is disrupted and that you become ruined by God's great love. As you keep your eyes on Jesus and draw near, may boldness come on you to step into a greater measure of your God-given destiny. As you are overcome and disarmed by His unyielding love, I pray that you fall more in love with Jesus than ever before, and that your courage will know no bounds.

1

The Secret Place

I love quiet and secluded places where I can get away from all distractions to give God my full attention. This way of life got heightened not many years ago. In early 2012, I moved into what would later become known as Destiny House. This home has since birthed a ministry made up of a tribe of worshipers who intentionally do life together and launch people into their destinies from a place of God's presence and through family. Shortly after I had moved in, I found myself in the midst of a storm. I had just received my Ph.D. and been ordained by one of my heroes, Heidi Baker, but I had no job, no car and no money, and nothing seemed to be coming together for me in my recent transition to Redding, California. This was the first time in my life I had to live off my credit card, which I hated. The doors I tried knocking on for employment all slammed shut in my face. I had no idea what to do or where to go. I just knew I needed to be closer to Jesus.

During this season, I found a way to go to a nearby lake, where I discovered a secret spot to be alone with Jesus each week. Throughout my times there, my only agenda was simply to be with Him. I did not have any answers, and I did not even know what to pray. I went to the lake in the morning without planning an ending time. I was with Him until I felt it was time to leave. Sometimes I would go for a swim, lie there, listen or simply just be. Other times, I would pray, journal, worship or read my Bible. It looked different every time. Sometimes I would hear Him speak to me, and other times it felt as if He were silent. The storm of lack and disillusionment I was facing led me there week after week.

If Jesus really is the way, the truth and the life (John 14:6), then I believed He was my way, He was my destination in the storm and He was my only answer. I had no other options but Him. Even before the answers came, being with Him in my storm brought peace, closeness and discovery of Him as my anchor still.

The desperation I experienced in the storm pressed me into a place of courage and risk-taking to step into what came next. Later that summer, God broke through in a special way with a job that I was born for. I eventually got back on my feet and started to move forward in life. God used this storm to stir up a greater hunger for Him and to help me cultivate a practice in my life that continues to this day.

Since making it through that hard time in 2012, I spend time at the lake each week with no other agenda than to simply "be" with Jesus. I get excited every time I drive to my secret spot on the lake's shore, because I know Jesus is there, waiting to spend time with me and commune together. He cannot wait to have me all to Himself. It has become a wonderful rhythm in my life.

While I was initially driven to the lake from a place of needing deliverance, a different sort of desperation now drives me. I am currently led to the lake each week because I am hungry to encounter more of His love and to be closer to Him. The circumstances are now irrelevant. Both in good and in difficult times, I need more of Jesus.

A New Song of Hope

During that same storm, when no doors were opening in my "Promised Land," a piano was given to us at Destiny House. I had learned to play the guitar in my teenage years, and though I had always admired the piano, I had not yet explored it. Since all I knew to do during that storm was to worship Jesus, I taught myself how to play.

It was during this season that I wrote my first worship song on the piano. I opened my Bible to Psalm 71, laid it on the piano and sang out the Scriptures. This song was my declaration that I would always have hope in God, even in the midst of storms. I knew I needed to worship Him no matter what the circumstances were. I knew I needed to declare hope into my situation even though I did not feel it at the time. I knew I could not let the storm raging around me steal my confidence in God. By my clinging to Him during that time, a new measure of courage and strength rose in me. My perspective rested upon the truth that God was good no matter what. The following was my heart's song and declaration of hope in that season:

> But as for me, I will always have hope
> And I will praise You more
> Till I come and declare Your works
> I will always have hope in You

Since my youth, You have taught me Your ways
Don't forsake me, Lord, till I come and declare Your
  works
I will always have hope in You

From making it through this hard season, several things became embedded in my spiritual DNA. Besides learning the significance of setting aside consistent time to be with God without any other agenda, I made a conscious decision that I would also worship Him no matter what storms came (as in 2 Chronicles 20). He is always faithful, and He never changes despite my circumstances. I learned that worship is a powerful weapon for the Kingdom of God that stills the storm inside of me even if a storm is thundering on the outside. I learned the profound truth that Jesus is always with me, both in good times and in bad.

Prayer Closet

Several years later, during the summer of 2015, I felt the Lord drawing me away to be with Him more than usual. I have had seasons like this throughout the years, when I felt a strong pull to get away with the Lover of my soul more often than normal. During these times, Jesus has allured me into greater levels of intimacy and relationship with Him in the secret place. This all required time.

During this season, I lived with my friends Tim and Nicol, and I responded to His leading by setting aside one of my closets solely for the purpose of encountering God. My little prayer closet was small but mighty, filled with glory! It was a place where I could play the guitar and worship as loud as I wanted, because no one in the house could really hear me. It was a place where I could leave my environment and pursue the "one thing" (see Psalm 27). It was a place set aside only for Him.

During this summer season, I felt led to give Him every morning in my prayer closet, singing melodies to Him as I strummed my guitar. These were special and sacred times. I did not do this because I wanted to prepare to do the impossible. I was not spending this time with Him so that I could step through major breakthroughs or do great miracles. I set aside this time and space simply to commune with the living God.

Developing Rhythms

One of the best ways to grow in our love and passion for God is by setting aside time to connect with Him regularly in the secret place. Jesus did this as a lifestyle. He developed a rhythm in which He prioritized meeting with His Father both in times of joy and in times of pain.

Not long before the story of Peter walking on water begins, Jesus learned that His friend John the Baptist had been killed. He responded to this news by withdrawing into a boat to be alone with His Father to process the grief. When He arrived on the other side of the lake, the multitudes found Him. He responded by healing their sick and by multiplying bread and fish to feed more than five thousand people (Matthew 14:1–21). After this miracle, the people were ready to force Him to become their king (John 6:14–15). Following this,

> Immediately Jesus made the disciples get into the boat and go on ahead of him to the other side, while he dismissed the crowd. After he had dismissed them, he went up on a mountainside by himself to pray. When evening came, he was there alone.
>
> Matthew 14:22–23

29

Jesus had just performed a miracle and had a powerful day of healing ministry, but even He needed to withdraw from the crowds to be alone with His Father. Whether He was celebrating miracles or continuing to grieve, Jesus regularly found refuge and life in communion with His Father.

Developing a secret place was an important part of Jesus' life. He often withdrew to lonely and secluded places to pray (Luke 5:16). To do this He would rise early in the morning while it was still dark (Mark 1:35). Jesus also had regular places where He would go and pray, like the Mount of Olives (Luke 22:39). He recognized that secret places could be cultivated in solitary settings as well as in the home (Matthew 6:6). Throughout His life, Jesus made it a priority and invested time again and again simply to be with His Father, and He encouraged others to follow His pattern.

Whenever Jesus came out of His times of solitude, He usually did something powerful or significant. After His forty-day fast in the wilderness, He was launched into His ministry (Mark 1:9–20). After spending the whole night on a mountainside to pray, the next day He chose His disciples (Luke 6:12–13). After Jesus came back from being alone, He miraculously fed the five thousand; then, after more time alone, He walked on water and stilled the storm (Matthew 14:13–33). The list could go on. Great exploits usually followed the time Jesus set apart to be with His Father.

If Jesus Himself needed time away from the crowds to thrive, and if He developed secret places to commune with God, then perhaps we need that, too. If we want to grow in our connection with God, we need to invest time with Him. Strong relationships are built on purpose, not by chance. Intimacy with Jesus requires time. This might cost us something. We might prefer to sleep in a little longer rather than wake up to fellowship with Him. Others might want to meet with us during our consecrated times to be with Him. We might have a to-do list screaming at us to get to work. But relationship with Jesus is worth fighting for. Time with Him is one of the most valuable investments we can make in this life.

While the end goal is to become a dwelling place where each of us can live in His presence every second of the day, no matter where we go, there is also something significant about setting aside a specific time and place to go deep with the One we love (Psalm 84). Union with God means being fully present. There is something about solitude and getting away from it all that helps bring better focus. When everything is stripped away and there are no distractions, we can give God our complete attention and hear His voice even more clearly. Both in good times and in bad, Jesus is waiting with open arms for us to run to Him in the secret place.

ACTIVATION: Developing Your Own Secret Place

1. Take a few minutes to ask the Holy Spirit to reveal to you a special place away from all distractions that can be set apart for union with Him. Write what He shows you below:

2. Now ask Him to show you an extended time each week that you can set apart, having no other agenda but simply to be with Him. Write this time below:

3. I encourage you to make it a point to regularly get away to be with Him in the time and place He just revealed to you. Allow Him to lead you. Ask Him to make you hungry for more of Him. Have no other agenda but simply to spend time with Him. You can even write in

your journal, "God, what do You want to speak to me today?" Then listen and write out what He shows you.

It pleases God's heart when we set aside time simply to commune with Him. When God answers our call for hunger, making time is easy because He regularly comes and apprehends us with His presence, where we cannot do anything but yield to Him. Making time to be vulnerable and to grow in intimacy with God is one of the most worthwhile investments we can make. Cultivating intimacy with Him is also an important foundation for stepping into and stewarding the impossible.

Be courageous to invite Him into areas of your heart left unexposed to His love. He wants to take you deeper today. He is good, He is safe and He will gently lead you beside still waters as you lean into Him and let Him love you.

2

Restoring Hope

While Jesus was prioritizing time in the secret place with His Father, His disciples were all alone in the middle of the lake, fending for their lives.

> Immediately Jesus made the disciples get into the boat and go on ahead of him to the other side, while he dismissed the crowd. After he had dismissed them, he went up on a mountainside by himself to pray. When evening came, he was there alone, and the boat was already a considerable distance from land, buffeted by the waves because the wind was against it.
>
> Matthew 14:22–24

Have you ever found yourself out there—all alone in the middle of turbulent and unsafe waters, simply because you followed the voice of Jesus? Does Jesus ever lead us into storms? And, if so, why would He do such a thing? At the beginning of the walking-on-water story in Matthew 14, it appears Jesus did just that. He specifically insisted that His disciples go to the other side of the lake while He disappeared to have some quiet time with His Father. The disciples obeyed the audible voice of Jesus to go in one direction, and before long a storm arose against them.

If I were to answer that question—Does Jesus ever lead us into storms?—I would have to say that the answer is sometimes yes. Sometimes He does lead us into dangerous waters, but it is always because He wants us to make it through to the other side. This process can be scary, painful, purifying and life defining. There is usually something beautiful on the other side of storms. Before Jesus began His ministry, He was *led* by the Spirit into the wilderness to be tempted by Satan (see Mark 1:12). This was a very uncomfortable and challenging time. Afterward, He stepped into His ministry with power.

If one is open to the idea that Jesus might at times lead us into storms, the other question that must be asked is why. I am not saying that Jesus causes bad things to happen to us, or that He wants storms to come into our lives in any way. In Romans 8:28, it says that *when* bad things happen, He turns them around for good to those who love Him and are called according to His purpose. Just because He turns the difficult circumstances around for the good does not make them any less bad. Storms are still turbulent, hard and painful. They are uncomfortable and dangerous. They strip us from any dependence we have on ourselves; they cause us to redefine our value systems and restructure our foundations. When we know it is Jesus leading us through the storm to the other side, however, we can trust that He will fulfill His purpose in the process.

Did I Really Hear God's Voice?

If you find yourself in a storm, it does not mean that you missed hearing God's voice. Sometimes when we follow what we believe to be the leading of the Holy Spirit, we encounter storms that hinder us from going where we feel God is calling us to go. When this happens, it can be easy to question if we heard from God in the first place.

Have you ever had a time when you set out by faith to follow God but then encountered resistance on the journey? In times of trouble, have you ever searched to find Jesus but discovered He was nowhere to be found? Or that He was silent? This might drive you to ask, *Where did Jesus go? I thought He called me here. Why does it feel like He has abandoned me? Maybe I didn't hear Him clearly. Maybe He didn't really call me to come here in the first place. I thought it would be smooth sailing, but the rough seas in the middle of the night are painful, and I don't like it at all.*

I have been there more than once. Many times I have felt the leading of the Holy Spirit to move in a certain direction only to end up in a storm, at a dead end or with a broken heart. These were disillusioning times that made me question if I had really heard from God to begin with. I used to be filled with questions and doubts until I came to realize that sometimes Jesus does lead us into storms, into difficult situations and to closed doors (Matthew 14; Isaiah 43:2; Acts 16:6–10). This usually happens because something great is waiting on the other side that requires perseverance. In other words, just because I was in a storm did not mean I did not hear God's voice. With this revelation, I was able to trust Him and myself more.

Disillusioned

In 2014, a home up the street from Destiny House was highlighted to me. I believed that this would be the perfect place to host missionaries who needed rest and refreshing and who would be able to walk to our worship meetings at Destiny House. The only thing was, it was not for rent but for sale. I had not thought of buying a house and I did not have any money to do so, but I still felt drawn to this home. Because I know that He is the God of the impossible, I stepped out in faith to meet with a lender who could set up a loan to see what might happen.

Over time I moved forward with this. On my birthday, February 18, 2014, I was at the library working on some of my writing when I felt compelled by the Holy Spirit to continue taking steps toward buying the house. I was not at peace or able to focus on anything else until I followed what I believed to be His leading.

As the days went on and I got closer to actually buying the home, I started to have doubts during the home inspection. I had several others join me on this adventure to give me advice whether I should move forward or not. Then, all of a sudden, everything began to shift. Excitement and anticipation gave way to concern over a few things wrong with the house. This caused some of my friends to caution me against buying it. Even with these red flags, I still tried to make something happen. At this point, however, as I attempted to move forward, I felt a disruption in my spirit, and my peace was taken away. I shifted into striving to make it fit because I thought I had felt the Lord leading me there. Finally, after a struggle, I ended up pulling out from buying the home and lost money on the inspection. The sellers ended up not selling the house but actually living in it, and I ended up staying where I was living for the time being. I was left confused and disillusioned by the whole thing.

Was it the Lord's will for me to buy the house at that time or just *pursue* buying the house? Was the timing off? I had tons of questions. I went as far as I could go with the Lord before I felt Him saying no. I have no regrets now because I was obedient to what I felt was His leading, even if the outcome was different from what I had imagined. In the process, I learned a lot about the steps to buying a home. I am grateful that, at the right time, the Lord will bring alignment.

Sometimes rejection is just redirection to something better. Other times rejection is a delay for something to come to pass at a different time. And sometimes it is God's protection. Understanding that there might be times when God actually does lead us into storms or to closed doors can restore our trust in Him and our trust in ourselves. What the enemy might want to use to destroy our lives, God can turn around to strengthen us.

As you read this, you might realize that you have become disillusioned because you have found yourself in the midst of a storm, even though you have been doing everything Jesus has asked of you. You might have stepped out in faith and as a result are struggling with debt, job transition, loss of your reputation, abandonment by those close to you or something else. None of it makes sense. If you have found yourself in the midst of a storm and are wondering how in the world you got there when all you were trying to do was follow the leading of the Holy Spirit, do not lose hope or condemn yourself. Suffering in the midst of a storm of life does not necessarily mean that you made a mistake, did not hear from God, were disobedient or went the wrong way. The disciples found themselves in a storm by being obedient to Jesus. I want you to know that you are still right in the center of His will for your life. Do not give up, doubt or second-guess yourself. You do not need to ask why or how this happened. Storms are storms, and sometimes they come out of nowhere. Jesus was not surprised when His disciples encountered the troublesome waters.

Deliverance

No matter how you found yourself in the storm, whether by trying to follow the leading of the Holy Spirit or by your own or others' mistakes, there is always hope for deliverance if you call out to God for help. Psalm 107 speaks of different people who found themselves in the "storms" of life, desperate to be rescued. Some of them were in bad situations as a result of disobedience; others had evil things happen to them; still others were simply pursing their destinies and got caught in one of the storms. The one commonality in all these situations was that when the people "cried out to the LORD in their trouble . . . he delivered them from their distress." He helped them no matter what brought them there in the first place—whether it was their fault or not.

Asking the question *why* in the midst of the storm will only cause further distress. According to Psalm 107, it does not really matter why or how one ends up in a horrible situation; the important thing to do is to seek God for deliverance. He will never let you down.

Getting to the Other Side

It was Jesus who made His disciples enter the boat and go ahead of Him to the other side. If Jesus tells you to cross to the other side of the lake, no matter what dangers or resistance might come along the way, He will be true to His word and get you there safely. There is something powerful about trusting in God and believing that what He has said will come to pass in our lives even if we have yet to see any of its fulfillment. Philippians 1:6 says that God will complete the good work He started in you. If God has put a dream or vision in your heart, He will give you the grace to fulfill it in His timing. Many times the resistance we face in the storms on the way to our God-commissioned destination is used to help refine, prepare, equip, release new authority and strengthen us to steward what is on the other side.

You may have received a prophetic word years ago or had a dream from God that has yet to be fulfilled. Sometimes it takes longer to reach our God-given destination than we expect because the dream is much bigger than we can imagine. Heidi Baker was called to go to Africa when she was only a teenager. She never gave up on this call of God, even though it took twenty years for her to first set foot in Mozambique. To this day, that whole country has been impacted by her *yes*. Storms, resistance and turbulence may all come in the journey, but if He said, *Go*, He will make sure we arrive in His time and in one piece.

ACTIVATION: **Restoring Hope**

1. If you are currently in a storm, I encourage you to pray this prayer out loud:

   God, I thank You that when I call out to You, You are ready to deliver me. I don't know how I ended up in this storm, but I ask that You would show Yourself faithful to enter into my current situation. Lord, come and still the rough waters that surround me. My arms are tired, and I'm exhausted from trying to keep my head above water. Would You enter into every area of my life with Your peace, strength and rest? I yield to You. Even in the midst of these painful circumstances that I don't understand, I choose to put my hope in You, to trust in Your promises that You are near. In every storm, You are my anchor still.

Thank You that there is something beautiful in the midst of this storm that You want to give me. Open my eyes to see the gold. Give me the courage to step into the breakthrough You have set before me. Where the enemy wants to use this storm to kill, steal and destroy, will You come and turn it around for good? Use this situation to make me stronger, purified like gold, more anointed to tear down strongholds. Change my perspective and help me to keep my eyes fixed on You. Let fearless worship and praise arise within me like never before. You are always faithful and worthy of all my praise. Thank You that You are with me and that You are always faithful.

2. If you feel that disillusionment from the storms of the past continues to hold you back, pray this prayer out loud:

Lord, I give You [name the situation or the person]. I feel like You didn't come through and that You left me hanging. I lost hope in You and in myself. Lord, forgive me for doubting You and myself just because I didn't understand. Forgive me for not trusting that even in the midst of that storm, You are good and You want the best for me. Even though I didn't understand what was going on at that time and I felt You were far from me, I ask You to come and show me now where You were in that storm.

Now wait on Him to discover where He was in the storm. Ask Him if He wants to give you anything new in exchange for the disillusionment, distrust, pain and hopelessness. Journal your response to how that makes you feel and what this means moving forward in your life, for taking risks again. Consider meeting with a friend to pray through this more.

I now bless you with hope that prevails, trust that is deeply rooted and peace that passes understanding. God is good and is for you even when circumstances do not seem to make any sense at all. You do hear from the Lord. Do not doubt yourself just because the outcome of obedience might have looked different from what you had imagined. God is with you, and He is proud of you for following His leading. May hope arise. May courage be imparted for you to receive the kindness of the Father in a new and greater measure. You are seen, chosen, fought for, understood and covered in the love of the Father. I bless you with healing, grace and fresh hope today in Jesus' name.

3

Peace in the Storm

If we have eyes to see, within each storm is an opportunity for God to do the impossible. Storms are pregnant with impending breakthroughs. Somewhere out there in the raging seas, Jesus is waiting for us to come to Him and walk on water. Somewhere in the depths of uncertainty stands Jesus, the way, the truth and the life (John 14:6). He is the way through the storms we are facing. He is all-powerful. He is always the answer.

If we can recognize Jesus in the midst of storms and keep our eyes on Him, peace will fill our hearts, and great courage to step into the impossible will be formed within us.

Resistance

As the disciples set out to obey the voice of Jesus and were halfway to their destination, they came up against resistance.[1] They struggled to move forward because of opposition from the wind and the waves: "When evening came, he was there

42

alone, but the boat was already a considerable distance from land, buffeted by the waves because the wind was against it" (Matthew 14:23–24).[2] The word *buffeted* is the Greek word *basanizo*, which means "to torture, torment, harass."[3] Buffeted is that moment when you have stepped out in utter dependence on God only to find yourself fending for your very life. It is when you have risked it all and have been vulnerable to obey His voice, only to be harassed by lies and accusations that you are not worth it or that you are not going to make it. It is the moment when you begin to question everything: *Did I really hear from the Lord? Did Jesus really send me in this direction? Maybe I thought it up all on my own. Is whatever is on the other side of this storm really going to be worth all this trouble? This journey is too hard; can I just give up?*

When we encounter resistance, it is usually because the Lord is forming something deep within us and is about to expand our territory. Our English word *resistance* stems from the Latin *resistere*, which means "to make a stand against, oppose."[4] *Resistance* can also refer to covert opposition to an occupying power. I have noticed in my own life that when lies and accusations come against me, when I am being harassed by the enemy and buffeted by the storms of life, it is because I am moving forward and taking new ground for Jesus. When I pause and ask the Lord what is really going on, usually I discover that it is an assault of the enemy over my life because I am expanding and occupying more territory for the Kingdom of God.

Terrified

In the midst of resistance and buffeting in the storm, the disciples came across another reason to fear: "During the fourth watch of the night Jesus went out to them, walking on the lake. When the disciples saw him walking on the lake, they were terrified. 'It's a ghost,' they said, and cried out in fear" (Matthew 14:25–26).

Already being tossed to and fro by the waves, the disciples saw what they perceived was a ghost, and they were terrified. The word *terrified* is the Greek word *tarasso*, which means "to agitate back-and-forth, to shake to-and-fro and to set in motion what needs to remain still."[5] It is interesting that the physical storm happening in the atmosphere around them entered into their hearts to cause an emotional storm carrying similar waves of fear. They did not yet have a strong anchor in the depths of their spirits to sustain rest and keep their minds still. They did not remember the time before when Jesus stilled the storm in their midst (Matthew 8:23–27). Instead, they allowed the outside storm to disrupt their inner peace.

Out of Context

The disciples, who had done life with Jesus, did not recognize Him out on the stormy sea because He appeared out of context. Jesus was right there in front of them, but they had allowed their environment to cloud their vision. Instead of hope arising because Jesus had arrived on the scene, fear crept in. Their surrounding circumstances polluted their ability to see, so much so that when they gazed on the face of Jesus, they thought He was a ghost.

When they could not identify Him standing right in front of them, He was gracious enough to speak to them, hoping that at least they would be able to recognize His voice. Immediately He said to them, "Take courage! It is I. Don't be afraid" (Matthew 14:27). Jesus *immediately* responded to their distress. His voice released truth that would open their eyes. He came with encouragement to set their hearts at ease.

Sometimes it might be easy to miss Jesus or even mistake Him for a ghost when we are in a storm. Our vision gets cloudy when things come against us. In those times when it is hard to see Him, it is good to open our ears to listen. There will be times when we cannot see what He is doing, but we will be able to hear Him. In times of fear or confusion, when we feel all alone in the dark, if we lean in to listen, we may hear Him say, *It is I—do not be afraid.* The hearing of a word from the Lord can open our eyes and give us peace, assurance and courage in a new way.

There are other times when we are desperate for God to show up or to hear a word from the Lord, but He appears to be hidden *and* silent. In those moments, we can still hope. When we cannot see Him or hear Him clearly in a storm, we can remember who He is and what He has done on our behalf in the past. We can encourage our hearts to trust in His faithfulness by remembering His incredible track record in our lives. The disciples had already watched Jesus still a storm earlier in their journey. By remembering what He had done in the past, they could have strengthened themselves in their present reality.

How Hope Catalyzed the Great Awakening

John Wesley, who would later go on to found the Methodist movement, was awakened to a new level of faith in the midst of a storm. In October 1735, he, along with his brother Charles and some friends, left England to go to America to bring the Gospel to the people there. While they were sailing to where they believed God had called them to go, they encountered a terrifying storm.

John and his friends feared for their lives. Because of their understanding of salvation at that time, they were not sure if they would make it to heaven if they died. While the British missionaries sat paralyzed with fear, the German Moravians on the boat sang praises and even held worship services in the midst of the storm. This caught John's attention. On Sunday, February 25, 1736, John wrote in his journal about what he saw:

> At noon our third storm began. At four it was more violent than before. At seven I went to the Germans. I had long before observed the great seriousness of their behaviour. Of their humility they had given a continual proof. . . . In the midst of the psalm wherewith their service began, the sea broke over, split the mainsail in pieces, covered the ship, and poured in between the decks, as if the great deep had already swallowed us up. A terrible screaming began among the English. The Germans calmly sung on. I asked one of them afterwards, "Was you not afraid?" He answered, "I thank God, no." I asked, "But were not your women and children afraid?" He replied, mildly, "No; our women and children are not afraid to die."[6]

John was dumbfounded by their steadfast faith in the midst of the storm. Even in the perilous conditions, they kept their eyes on Jesus. God remained their anchor. They all eventually made it through this storm safely, and John was marked in a profound way. He continued to cultivate friendship with the Moravians and went on to have a defining moment when his "heart was strangely warmed" in conjunction with this group. Not long after, he was catalytic in helping birth the Great Awakening and then the Methodist movement. The Moravians' focus on Jesus in the storm awakened John to a new level of faith that would eventually impact the face of Christianity as we know it.

See Jesus in the Storm

God is always at work, even in the midst of storms. There is something valuable to be discovered in the dark places (Isaiah 45:2–4). Somewhere hidden beneath a relational conflict is a gem waiting to be discovered. Somewhere buried under the mountain of debt we face is a pearl of great price. Somewhere in the midst of confusion is a peace that passes understanding (Philippians 4:4–7). Somewhere in the storm are keys we need to discover that will equip us for what lies on the other side.

If we are anchored in Jesus, we will not be shaken when a storm comes. True leaders arise when faced with resistance. God can use the turbulence in our lives to strengthen us. Sometimes storms can be used to open our eyes to see Jesus as never before and help us find Him even in the hard places. I have learned that something happens in a storm that gives us an opportunity to break into greater levels of intimacy with God, as well as increased authority, anointing, determination and courage. These are some questions I have learned to ask myself in the midst of the storm:

- Where is Jesus in this storm?
- What great breakthrough is the Lord inviting me to step into that the enemy is trying to distract me from?
- What is God preparing me for on the other side?
- Is there anything God wants to heal in me, or are there any lessons I need to learn that can only be developed by persevering through the storm?
- What miracle is waiting to happen as I keep my eyes on Jesus?

ACTIVATION: Walking in Peace

As I was writing this chapter, I felt that God would set people free who have felt tormented in their minds. Maybe you have been plagued with fear and anxiety or have had sleepless nights. Maybe your mind is bombarded with lies and accusations from the enemy. You are not alone in your present situation. Take courage; you are on the verge of a great breakthrough. Invite Jesus to come and manifest His presence exactly where you are today. Welcome Him to come and still the storm you are facing. Jesus is going to set you free right now. If this describes you, repeat after me:

I renounce fear, anxiety, torment and any and all harassing spirits in Jesus' name. I rebuke any assaults and cancel any generational curses over my life. I silence the lies and accusations of the enemy. Only the truth of Jesus is welcome in my life. I forgive and release [anyone whom the Lord brings to mind] for [name anything done against you], and bless [name of the person] with the Father's love. I pray that Your goodness will overtake [name of the person]. I command the peace that passes understanding to guard my heart and my mind in Christ Jesus.

I declare that I am a steward of peace and that God is my anchor who stills every storm. I am powerful, and I have authority to walk in truth and peace. God is my protector. I am safe with Him always. I receive His peace right now. I choose to walk in courage toward Jesus and all that He has called me to do and to become. I am a child of God, chosen, pursued and fought for. Jesus has paid the ultimate price for me. I choose to receive the fullness of His love. I invite the Holy Spirit to come with a fresh baptism of peace. I receive the Father's covering of love and protection in my life. I am free in Christ Jesus and

covered in His blood. I will walk in peace and will keep my
eyes on Jesus. I choose to worship Him no matter what storms
or resistance come my way, because He is always faithful and
worthy of my praise.

I now pronounce that you are forgiven, set free and full of
peace in Jesus' name. May the commanding peace that passes
understanding guard your heart and mind in Christ Jesus.
Where the enemy has come to kill, steal and destroy, especially at night or in your thought life, I declare a shift in Jesus'
name. I call for heavenly visions, dreams and encounters to
be released in the night seasons and for the blood of Jesus to
cover and protect you completely. May the Lord sing songs
of deliverance over you. You are now a carrier of peace in
Jesus' name.

Tips for Stewarding Peace through Storms

Below are a few practical suggestions that I practice in my
life to steward peace in the midst of storms. I pray that these
will help you continue to walk in peace no matter what resistance comes up against you.

1. Regardless of the circumstances, worship God because
   He is worthy (2 Chronicles 20).
2. Praise Him for His character and nature, focusing on
   the opposite of what you are facing. (For example, if
   you are struggling with lack, praise Him for being your
   provider. If you are hopeless, praise Him for being a
   God of hope.)
3. Practice thanksgiving (1 Thessalonians 5:16–18). Reflect
   on moments in the past when God came through in a
   similar situation. Thank Him for His faithfulness in

those situations, and also thank Him ahead of time that He is going to get you through this storm.

4. Trust that God is good, is for you and is working behind the scenes on your behalf to bring you into a greater measure of abundance as you press into Him (Romans 8).

5. Call or meet up with a friend to pray through and process what is going on in your head and heart.

6. Exercise and meditate on His goodness during that time.

7. Realize that this storm will not last forever and that you are on the verge of a great breakthrough. On the other side of the storm is something special. Let your worship, dance and prayers be even more fierce. Gather friends to worship and press in together.

The following verses are also great to meditate on in relation to this theme:

> Rejoice in the Lord always. I will say it again: Rejoice! Let your gentleness be evident to all. The Lord is near. Do not be anxious about anything, but in everything, by prayer and petition, with thanksgiving, present your requests to God. And the peace of God, which transcends all understanding, will guard your hearts and your minds in Christ Jesus. Finally, brothers, whatever is true, whatever is noble, whatever is right, whatever is pure, whatever is lovely, whatever is admirable—if anything is excellent or praiseworthy—think about such things. Whatever you have learned or received or heard from me, or seen in me—put it into practice. And the God of peace will be with you.
>
> Philippians 4:4–9

4

The Art of Letting Go

As soon as Peter's nerves were calmed enough to recognize that it was Jesus on the waters, he immediately wanted to be closer to Him. Once he got the okay from Jesus, he was ready to go for it. But before Peter could take his first step into the impossible, he had to come to the place of total surrender: He had to let go of the boat. "'Lord, if it's you,' Peter replied, 'tell me to come to you on the water.' 'Come,' he said. Then Peter got down out of the boat, walked on the water and came toward Jesus" (Matthew 14:28–29).

Can you imagine what that must have felt like? Climbing over the side of the boat in the midst of a storm and letting go? The moment he let go of the boat, he stepped into a completely new realm of faith. He had nothing to cling to for safety in the turbulent waters. As he let go, his only option became Jesus. Peter had no backup plan. He put himself out there in the most vulnerable and dangerous position possible. If Jesus had not sustained him, he could have drowned. What a beautiful act of surrender and trust Peter demonstrated when he let go of the boat and relied completely on Jesus.

I once had a blog with this title: *Letting Go. To Embrace the Struggle. To Live Loudly.* Surrender—sometimes it feels like a natural and necessary progression on the journey to living wholeheartedly. A seed has to fall to the ground and die before it can release new life (see John 12:24). Something powerful happens when we finally surrender, give up and let go.

When we let go of control and are fully able to trust Jesus, we allow Him to carry us and we become transformed. Freedom and breakthrough are on the other side of surrendering every ounce of control, self-reliance, pride and independence simply to be nearer to Jesus. Stepping into the abyss of uncertainty and risking it all to be closer to Jesus is one of the scariest, most nerve-wracking and most beautiful journeys of vulnerability one could venture on.

Madame Jeanne Guyon (1648–1717), who gave her life to pursue deep intimacy with Jesus, said, "Great faith produces great abandonment."[1] This makes complete sense. Great faith is tied to total surrender, releasing all control and stepping off the boat.

Sweet Surrender

I recently discovered the life of a missionary who surrendered everything to serve the broken and the lost. Lilias Trotter (1853–1928) grew up in London and poured out her life for Jesus by loving those less fortunate. She was known to venture out late at night by herself to rescue prostitutes off the streets of London.[2]

Lilias was also an anointed artist and had the opportunity to make a career out of it. Instead of choosing the path of a successful artist, as famous art critics recommended she do, she felt she needed to focus on reaching the lost people of northern Africa with the love of Jesus. She surrendered her wealth, talents and desires so she could give her life for the unreached people in Algeria. After mission boards rejected her application to be a missionary, with her own money she decided to pioneer to bring Jesus to the people in northern Africa. For forty years she lived among the nationals, serving them in the hiddenness of the desert. Lilias's life was a deep well. She was an inspiring artist, writer, pioneer, missionary and lover of Jesus who lived a life of surrender.

Another woman who knew what it was like to abandon everything to the will of God was a prominent leader in the Divine Healing movement and early Pentecostalism, Carrie Judd Montgomery (1858–1946). As a teenager, Carrie dreamed of becoming a teacher and writer, but she surrendered her dream to the Lord after a very painful sickness that nearly took her life. After she was miraculously healed, God resurrected her dream and caused her to write books that even today continue to release God's healing to those who read them. She was used to establish some of the earliest healing homes in the nation, including the Home of Peace in Oakland, California, in 1893, which is there to this day.[3]

Heidi Baker (born 1959), present-day missionary to Africa, had a dream when she was young to be a ballerina. Once she encountered God's love, she felt led to lay down her ballet shoes so she could be fully devoted to Him. She has since gone on to greatly impact the nation of Mozambique and the world by her yes to Jesus. God resurrected her passion for dance and has allowed her to release it in worship and before His throne. God has done far beyond what she could have imagined since she surrendered all for Him.[4]

The talents these women submitted to the Lord were not bad endeavors at all. They simply felt that at one time in their lives these passions could have taken a greater priority over Jesus. In acts of obedience, they surrendered even these good talents to God. He has since used their lives to spread the Gospel around the world and to pioneer into new territories, many times using their once-surrendered gifts in a greater way. Just because God sometimes calls us to lay down things that are precious to us does not in any way mean that these things are bad. It has more to do with letting Him take first place in our hearts and yielding to Him in all situations.

Total Consecration

When I think about this theme of letting go, total surrender and abandonment to Jesus, the story of Rees Howells (1879–1950) also comes to mind. Howells was born in Wales and became a part of the great Welsh revival of 1904–1905 led by Evan Roberts. Such a massive outpouring of the Spirit of God fell on Wales that in less than four months more than a hundred thousand people got saved. Howells had a powerful encounter after he was already a Christian that led him to a lifestyle of total abandonment and deeper consecration (being fully set apart for God's purposes).

In 1906, when Howells was 26 years old, he went to a conference in Llandrindod Wells, where he heard a minister talk about being fully possessed by the Holy Spirit. This opened him up to see the Holy Spirit with fresh eyes.[5] During that meeting, he felt that God invited him into a place of unconditional surrender and complete possession of the Holy Spirit. He was given five days to give God the answer to His request.

Immediately following that service, Howells went into a field and called out to God. He wept for days over this decision to surrender all to God and lost seven pounds in the process. He knew that once he agreed to total surrender, it was for life; there would be no going back. For five days he was alone with God, mulling over this decision. He understood that God was not going to

> take any superficial surrender. He put His finger on each part of my self-life, and I had to decide in cold blood. . . . It was a breaking, and the Holy Ghost taking control. Day by day the dealing went on. He was coming in as God, and I had lived as a man, and "what is permissible to an ordinary man," He told me, "will not be permissible to you."[6]

On the fifth day, Howells heard the Spirit say,

> "I have been dealing with you for five days; you must give Me your decision by six o'clock tonight and remember, your will must go. On no account will I allow you to bring in a crosscurrent. Where I send you, you will go; what I say to you, you will do."[7]

He was not ready to make the decision, so he asked for more time, but he felt God answer, "At six o'clock I will take your decision. After that you will never get another chance."[8] He was being called up higher. He recalled,

> My will would have to go; I would never have another choice, and I was never to question him in thought, word or motive. Each day he cleansed and purged me so that I could never go back again to my former life, and finally he gave me one hour to decide whether I, myself, was to live on, or he was to live in me. My destiny for eternity depended on that hour.[9]

At 5:59 p.m. on the fifth day, with not a moment more to spare, Howells surrendered himself to the Lord. He gave the Holy Spirit full control and total possession:

> At last I said, "Lord, I am willing," and he came in. He did not force the decision on me: I had to decide. I was carried right into the presence of God and the verse he gave me was: "Having therefore, brethren, boldness to enter into the holiest by the blood of Jesus" (Hebrews 10:19). From that time on there was a line drawn between my old life and this new one.[10]

Right after he made this act of surrender and consecration, he felt the Holy Spirit rush in. He remembered being "transported to another realm," where God spoke to him.[11] The same night he made this surrender, the presence of God invaded the house where Howells met with a small gathering of believers, and they sang the same chorus, "There's power in the blood," for two hours straight. God continued to speak things to him he "had never dreamed of" before into the early hours of the morning.[12]

When Fire Falls on the Sacrifice

Following this encounter, Howells was led into a lifestyle of extreme consecration and surrender. He took on a Nazirite type of vow for a season, during which he fasted two meals each day. He also set aside three hours every night, from 6:00 to 9:00 p.m., to commune with God. During this time, he would read the Bible for two hours and remain in silence for an hour, waiting on God, all while on his knees. He recalled,

> Although we may be away from the presence of people, how hard it is to silence the voices of self. But after a time the Lord brought me to the place where the moment I shut the

door at six o'clock, I left the world outside and had access into the presence of God.[13]

Howells invited the Holy Spirit to possess him so fully that one time someone came to town who did not know his name and "simply asked the ticket collector at the station where 'the man with the Holy Ghost' lived and was directed to Mr. Howells!"[14]

Howells's act of complete surrender and letting go of his own wants and desires was multiplied through his disciples. He later felt called to start a ministry school where "young people might come to learn a life of faith, and above all be filled with the Holy Spirit."[15] With only fifteen cents to his name, Howells stepped into the impossible to purchase a building for this school. As he continued to pray and press in to believe God for the fulfillment of this dream, several small donations regularly arrived just before the payments were due to purchase the building. Howells was able to launch the school in 1924 with 5 teachers and 38 students.[16]

Years later, in early 1937—just over nine months after Howells called the school to an act of total consecration in which the fire of God fell in a powerful way—another outpouring of the Spirit was released. During a prayer meeting, one of his staff broke down "confessing her sense of need and crying to the Holy Spirit to meet her."[17] After this happened, a beautiful outpouring of the Spirit filled the school. The headmaster at the time recalled that God

> did not come like a rushing mighty wind. But gradually the person of the Holy Ghost filled all our thoughts, His presence filled the place, and His light seemed to penetrate all the hidden recesses of our hearts. He was speaking through the Director in every meeting, but it was in the quiet of our own rooms that He revealed Himself to many of us.

> We felt the Holy Spirit had been a real Person to us before; as far as we knew we had received Him; and some of us had known much of His operations in and through our lives. But now the revelation of His Person was so tremendous that all our previous experiences seemed as nothing. There was no visible apparition, but He made Himself so real to our spiritual eyes that it was a "face to face" experience. And when we saw Him we knew we had never really seen Him before. . . .
>
> We were people who had left all to follow the Savior, and had forsaken all we had of this world's goods to enter a life of faith, and as far as we knew we had surrendered our lives entirely to the One who died for us. But He showed us, "There is all the difference in the world between *your* surrendered life in My hands, and Me living *My* life in your body."[18]

Howells and his students realized that surrendering was just the beginning. It was incomplete without their asking the Holy Spirit to come and fully possess them.

At just 26 years of age, Howells was given a choice to fully surrender and let go of his life and invite the Holy Spirit to come and inhabit him. His personal act of surrender and of abandoning his life to Jesus no matter what the cost has marked many lives and will continue to mark generations to come. Since his death in 1950, thousands have been trained and sent out to the nations from Howells's school, including a German missionary named Reinhard Bonnke, who attended the college in the 1950s.[19] Since his time there Bonnke has brought well over seventy million people into the Kingdom and continues to evangelize around the world.

Rees Howells was called to a different level of surrender and consecration than most. Similarly, Peter's action to step outside the boat was extreme. No one around him even thought of doing something like that. Some people are called to make greater sacrifices, take greater risks, pay a greater price and walk in greater levels of holiness than others. Just because others are not stepping out of a boat you feel you are supposed to step out of does not mean that you cannot or should not.

Some of you reading this are called to pioneer into new arenas that others are not called to and might not understand. You might be called to let go of the comforts of society or to step out in faith toward something that has never been done before. Do not listen to accusations of the enemy or worry about offending others. The most important thing is to follow the leading of the Holy Spirit and live from your heart to do whatever it takes to meet Jesus in the deeper places. At the same time, we should realize that just because the other disciples did not get out of the boat with Peter does not mean that their lives were less valuable or in any way insignificant; it just means that they had a different calling and a different path to get there.

Not everyone was willing to let go of all inhibitions and step outside the boat to be with Jesus. But Peter was, and so are you called to do things that no one else has ever done. As long as you keep your eyes on Jesus and move in forward momentum toward Him, you will go places you have never dreamed of in Him.

ACTIVATION: **Letting Go**

When Peter let go of the boat, he gave up his right to be in control. He yielded to and trusted Jesus with his whole heart. He left behind the place of refuge, safety and security so he could move toward the One who was abundant life Himself.

Surrender looks different in all circumstances, and sometimes the hardest things to surrender are not things at all. It might mean letting go of a toxic relationship in one situation by repositioning your life and setting healthy boundaries. In another situation, surrender might look more like letting go of control and surrendering completely to God the person or thing you have allowed to take a higher place in your heart. Sometimes surrender looks like taking action to cut off what is destructive, and other times it has more to do with a heart stance of being yielded to Him.

1. What or who are some of the "boats" in your life that you are hanging on to for security?

2. Do you have anything or anyone in your life that you are elevating above Jesus or running to before running to Him?

3. What or whom do you need to let go of, surrender and entrust to the Lord today so that you can venture out into even deeper waters to be closer to Jesus?

    Jesus longs to satisfy us completely and be the well we run to for living water. Once we let go and surrender competing lovers, we also need to invite Jesus to inhabit and fully possess us. Jesus is our fortress. He is the One who fully satisfies and meets our deepest needs. Spend some time journaling and surrendering your life afresh to Jesus. Invite the Holy Spirit to come and possess and fill you with more of His love. Trust that He wants the very best for your life. He is worth any sacrifice you feel He is asking you to make today. Let's make a fresh consecration, yielding our wills before the Lord today. Declare the following with me:

    > You can have it all, Lord. I give You my every thought, my every breath, my every desire. All I am is Yours. Nothing

else matters but knowing You more. If there is anything or any relationship in my life that I am placing above You, even if it is good, bring Your refining fire. Put things in their proper order. Bring perfect alignment in every area of my heart. Help me to refocus my affection on You. You are worth my whole heart, not just a portion of it. If anything is too hard for me to surrender to You on my own, I invite You to come and take it away. I trust You with my whole heart. I surrender all into Your hands. Enter in to fully possess me with Your love. Let my life be a holy habitation where You are welcome to come and dwell. Today I declare that I am all in, and that my heart is fully Yours.

5

Compelled by Love

Peter risked everything to step into the impossible to be closer to Jesus. He threw out rational thinking and any sort of wisdom. He threw off all inhibitions and was led by raw adrenaline, impulsivity and passion. He was willing to put himself into greater danger to be with the One he loved. It did not make any sense. In the boat, at least he was somewhat safe. To leave that security to go into dangerous waters toward a friend who was defying the laws of nature is madness. Even more, thinking that he could do the same as Jesus was ludicrous.

Have you ever noticed that being in love can make people do crazy things? It seems like barriers dissolve into nothing when love is thrown into the equation. When we know we are loved, we will do anything.

From the day Peter had first encountered Jesus, he was compelled to follow Him anywhere, even at times into greater danger. Peter's passion to be closer to Jesus superseded his fear of the surrounding circumstances. He trusted in Jesus' authority and knew that if He gave the command to walk on water, then it could be done. The reason Peter could do something so extreme was because he had an understanding of the love of Jesus. In his first interaction with Jesus, Peter found what his heart had been yearning for his whole life, so he dropped everything. He let go of his dreams, aspirations, self-sufficiency and comfort to follow a man who made everything inside of him come alive and who gave him purpose.

Jesus

What was it about Jesus that compelled Peter to get out of a boat and put himself in greater danger to be near Him? Let's look at the backstory of their relationship and how they first met.

In Matthew 4:18–19, Jesus was walking beside the sea, and when He saw Peter, He called him to be one of His first disciples. "Come, follow me," Jesus said, "and I will make you fishers of men." Peter was seen, chosen and given an opportunity to make a difference in the world. At once, Peter and his brother Andrew dropped their nets to follow this great teacher.

In Luke 5:1–11, we are able to go behind the scenes of this decision to learn what initially inspired Peter to leave everything to follow Jesus in that moment. Jesus was at the water's edge, next to two boats—one of which was Peter's—speaking to the crowds about the Word of God. After a whole night of fishing with nothing to show for it, Peter and his brother left their boat to wash their nets. Meanwhile Jesus decided to make Himself at home in Peter's boat. After Jesus asked Peter to put out a little from the shore, He sat down in the boat and continued to teach the people.

First of all, this is an interesting introduction. It might sound like Jesus was hijacking Peter's boat without asking him. On the other hand, what an honor that Jesus chose Peter's boat to inhabit! This great teacher saw something in Peter; He even felt comfortable enough to fill his space. After Jesus had finished teaching, He told Peter, who at that time was still called Simon, to go into deep water and let his net down for a catch. This was after Peter had been out all night unsuccessfully fishing and had already cleaned the nets. Luckily for Peter, because it was Jesus who said it, he obeyed and did it His way this time.

When Peter and Andrew followed Jesus' instructions, they caught so many fish that their nets began to break. They had to call for their partners in the other boat—none other than brothers James and John—to come quickly to help them with the abundance of fish that was coming to them. Both boats were so full of fish that they began to sink! By responding to one word from Jesus, in a moment they experienced a breakthrough. The result was a true financial miracle.

After this impossibility became reality before his eyes, Peter ran to Jesus and fell at His feet. He did not know how to handle all of the love and favor from this great teacher. Instead of receiving this blessing of abundance, he cried, "Go away from me, Lord; I am a sinful man!" (Luke 5:8). He had his eyes on his own frailty and weakness rather than on Jesus. Because of his insecurity and not feeling valuable enough, he chose to reject the giver of the blessing rather than embrace Him. Peter's statement was all about him, full of pride and self-pity clothed in false humility. He partnered with shame and struggled to receive this incredible gift from Jesus because he was too focused on himself. He was afraid of being seen, known, loved and fully received. When the love got too strong to handle, he pushed Jesus away.

Thankfully, Peter's bold rejection did not offend Jesus. His love continued to break through the shame even into the hardest of hearts. In this moment, Jesus could have given up on Peter and let him go. He could have chosen someone else to invite into His intimate circle of friends. Instead, He said, "Don't be afraid; from now on you will catch men" (Luke 5:10). Jesus saw Peter's greater purpose beyond his insecurities. Though Peter still saw himself as a struggling fisherman, Jesus saw his true identity as a rock that God would later build his Church upon. Peter and the others responded to this love by pulling their boats to shore and then leaving everything to follow Jesus.

Found

I remember the first time I encountered Jesus in a profound way. I grew up in a Christian family and had always known *about* Jesus from going to church. When I was a child, I had accepted Jesus into my heart more than once at my school's chapel services. I had always stayed away from the "bad stuff" as a kid; I did not drink, have sex or do drugs. But staying away from the "bad stuff" did not mean I had a personal relationship with Jesus. I believed in Him, obeyed the "rules" and went to church. I was good at going through the motions, but I do not remember experiencing Him in an intimate way.

I was extremely shy as a kid. I attended a small Christian school with only six or so other students in my class. There, I was fine. But when I graduated and transferred to a junior high school down the street with more than seventy people in my grade, I was overwhelmed with all the new people. I was twelve years old; I did not know anyone in the new school, and I struggled to make friends. I tried to hang out in different groups but never seemed to fit in. Besides being shy, I was a little overweight and had buckteeth from sucking

65

my thumb way too long. I could never quite figure out the fashion thing, and growing up I had been a tomboy, climbing trees and playing sports with the boys.

Lunchtimes were the worst. It was a set amount of time with no structure and no order, when everyone could sit wherever they wanted and had the freedom to pick and choose their friends. At least in the classrooms, we had assigned seats and I felt safe with a teacher there. When the bell rang, however, I became a social outcast. There was no stability for me during the lunch period. I had nothing to hold on to.

One time during lunch, I worked up the courage to try to make friends with a clique of girls sitting at a table. When I approached the table, one of them said, "We don't want you here." The interesting thing is that I still remember this girl's first and last name to this day. I was crushed, and rejection set in. What was wrong with me? I called my sister on the pay phone almost daily with tears, begging her to help me get out of the school. I felt as if I were drowning. I could not see God in my situation anywhere. I felt all alone.

My parents kept me in that school against my pleas to leave, although I knew it must have been a hard decision for them. In retrospect, I am thankful they allowed me to persevere. My eighth-grade year went a little better because I was good at sports and was able to make a few friends that way. But a similar thing happened when I became a freshman in high school: I transitioned to a public school and my class size more than tripled. I was overwhelmed in the sea of students.

Again I tried to find friends; again I never seemed to fit in with any crowd. Sometimes it was not even them rejecting me; it was me not finding anyone I wanted to get to know because I felt different from everyone else. Toward the end of the year, I finally gave up trying; I started going into the girl's locker room during the lunch period. No one would be able to see my loneliness there. In that secure place, I could hide and disappear.

There, in the midst of this long storm, as I sat all alone, I began reading the Bible. God's Word came alive to me like never before. As I read it day after day, I discovered that Christianity was not about what *not* to do; it was about living, it was about loving, it was about a Man named Jesus who was passionately in love with me. I finally understood that Christianity was not just about keeping the Ten Commandments; it was about how God loved me enough to sacrifice His only Son in exchange for my life. I understood that God was not looking down at me, waiting for me to make a mistake so He could punish me, but that He could not keep His eyes off me because He was so in love with me.

In this storm of loneliness, I began to see Jesus—to *really* see Him—for the first time. I began to understand the love He had for me: that He would live His whole life on earth for just one purpose—to die for me! Instead of watching me walk to hell because I would never be good or holy enough to see God on my own, He took my place, He took away my sins and He shed His own blood so that I would not have to. Each day He walked one step closer to death with me on His mind. He gladly and willingly laid down His life so He could see me face-to-face.

God used these storms in junior high and high school to draw me to Him. By my senior year of high school, I had friends in almost every social group, and I even got voted "Friendliest" because I had learned how to be a friend to those in need. Reading the Bible was a key to seeing Jesus more clearly and falling in love with Him for the first time. Rather than Christianity being mere religion, it was transformed into a passionate love affair with the person Jesus.

After I discovered the real Jesus in that profound way, I knew I wanted to give Him my whole life. I was all in.

All In

From Peter's first interaction with Jesus, he had been marked by His unrelenting love. He had been singled out and chosen to become great. From that day on, he was all in. Being a fisherman was not regarded as a prestigious profession. With Jesus in his life now, Peter had been given an opportunity to become something great, to do something significant with his life. There was hope in Jesus' eyes, the promise of destiny.

Jesus met Peter exactly where he was, even making His home with him. He began with a miracle in Peter's workplace, blessing him where his heart would understand the most. Not long after, Jesus went into Peter's home, where He healed his mother-in-law, who lay in bed with a fever (Mark 1:30–31). Jesus cared about the things important to Peter, including his business and his family. He was patient while Peter worked things out in his own heart in the process of learning to follow Him.

As one of Jesus' very first disciples, Peter got to see most of Jesus' ministry from the beginning. He watched Jesus turn water into wine, cast out demons, heal the sick and raise the dead. In a previous boat ride, Peter saw Jesus rebuke the wind and the waves, which shifted the atmosphere and brought complete calm over the waters (Matthew 8:23–27). Sound familiar? This was not just any teacher Peter wanted to meet in the midst of the storm; He was the One who had authority over the wind and the waves, which Peter had previously witnessed firsthand.

There was something about this Man named Jesus that compelled Peter to want to do the unthinkable, the impossible. Jesus had already changed Peter's life; He set him free from shame and made him feel safe. When Peter encountered the love of Jesus, he was wrecked for anything else. He was all in. Where else could he go? Jesus alone had the words of life. His destiny was found in this friend. This was the mark Jesus had made on Peter's life. Even before Peter had become a great leader, Jesus accepted and loved him for who he was. Jesus had stepped inside of Peter's boat the day they met; now He welcomed Peter to step outside the boat.

ACTIVATION: Receiving God's Unrelenting Love

1. If you have yet to encounter the love of Jesus as I described earlier, and you want to know Him in a more intimate and personal way, I encourage you to call out to Him in your own words. Invite Him to come into your heart in a deeper way than before. He will meet you exactly where you are today. You do not need to try to get cleaned up before coming to Him. He loves you just as you are today and would love to get to know you more.

2. We all have God stories that are unique and significant. It is important to recall what God has done in the past to be reminded of His saving grace and also to share with others to release hope. I encourage you to process the answers to these questions and write out your own story:

   How did you first encounter the love of Jesus?

   Who is Jesus to you, and how has He already impacted your life?

3. When Jesus first met and then blessed Peter with abundance, Peter struggled to receive love because he was focused on his own insecurities. The courage Peter later demonstrated existed because he had allowed the love of Jesus to melt down the walls of shame. Reflect on the following questions:

How do you feel when God or others bless you? Are you openhearted to receive favor, blessing and abundance? Or do you feel unworthy when God chooses to lavish these upon you, because of shame? If so, where is your focus?

How would you feel if you had already paid a great price to give someone a gift and that person did not want to receive it because he or she felt unworthy?

If you are able to freely receive His blessings, praise the Lord! I pray that God expands your heart to receive and to give even more away. If you feel blocked by shame from the past or do not feel like you deserve the goodness of God, I encourage you to ask the Holy Spirit to reveal why that is and welcome Him to work deeper in you. You cannot carry shame and walk on water at the same time. Ask for forgiveness for not receiving what Jesus has already paid to give you. Open wide your heart to receive all that God has for you today. Renounce any shame in your life. Remember that today is a new day and that He makes all things new. Your sin is separated as far as the east is from the west. No failure or mistake is too big to be able to separate you from the love of God (Romans 8). Freely receive His grace, blessings, favor and goodness today. You can also pray this prayer out loud as you feel led:

God, I repent of any ways that I have partnered with shame. I renounce shame, guilt and condemnation in my life in Jesus' name. I renounce the lie that I am unworthy to receive Your love. I believe the truth that I am significant and that there is now no condemnation for those who are in Christ Jesus (Romans 8:1–2). Forgive me for not fully trusting in Your goodness or receiving the gift of intimate friendship that You have already died to pay for. Forgive me for trying to earn Your love. Purify my heart and position me to receive Your grace and mercy in overflowing measures. Thank You that You never stop pursuing me. Thank You that You never give up on me. Thank You that You have already paid the ultimate price to love me. Thank You that nothing from my past can hinder my future in You. Today I receive Your persistent, enduring and unrelenting love. Today I choose to partner with the truth that I am valuable and important because You have set Your love upon me. I welcome, invite and receive Your love in the deepest places of my heart today. Holy Spirit, come and overshadow me with the Father's love and embrace. Mark me with Your healing love. Thank You that I am safe in You.

I pray that even now you are overshadowed with the love, acceptance and forgiveness of Jesus like never before. You are worth it. He has already paid the ultimate price. Receive the love that has been freely given so that you can overflow to a world that is desperate to receive His love through you. May His love compel you to a place of total surrender and courage to risk. May the walls of shame be completely melted away as you fix your eyes on Jesus and receive His impenetrable love. May your passion to be closer to Jesus ignite a new revolution of love that impacts those around you and generations to come.

6

Focus

As long as Peter kept his eyes on Jesus, he continued to do the impossible. One of the keys to walking in the miraculous is keeping our focus on Jesus and getting our courage from Him. Despite circumstances that try to steal our hope, we must remain focused on the face of Jesus always. When we do this, no matter what storms rage around us, we will have peace that passes understanding, and many times we will do the impossible without necessarily even trying. Focusing on Jesus in all circumstances refines our hearts and ignites the fire of God within us like never before.

Fire

The word *focus* is rooted in fire. In the early 1600s, scientists chose the Latin word *focus* to name the point at which sunlight converges in a magnifying glass to start a fire.[1] In postclassical times, the word *focus* was even used for fire itself. The Latin word *focus* also meant "hearth" or "fireplace," which figuratively can represent home and family.[2] This is not surprising, as family is what truly houses the focused fire of revival.

Focus ignites. It can lead to synergy and alignment in a more powerful and accelerated way than before. By simply giving Jesus our full attention, convergence for breakthrough happens in a catalytic way. If in the natural focus can ignite fire, can you imagine what could happen when our fiery gaze remains on the Savior?

One Thing

What we focus on shapes our lives and determines who we will become. There is power and safety in focusing all of our attention on the one thing, Jesus Himself. In Psalm 27, even when chaos and war were breaking out all around him, David fought to keep his focus on the one thing:

> Though an army besiege me, my heart will not fear; though war break out against me, even then will I be confident. *One thing* I ask of the LORD, this is what I seek: that I may dwell in the house of the LORD all the days of my life, to gaze upon the beauty of the LORD and to seek him in his temple.
>
> Psalm 27:3–4, emphasis mine

In the midst of war, impending destruction and great distraction, the psalmist set his heart to dwell in God's presence and to gaze upon Him. That is all he wanted, and it was all that really mattered to him. Even though he was the king of a nation, with pressures on all sides and a to-do list longer than most of us will ever know, his one and only and most important objective was to dwell in God's presence. That was the safest place he could put himself.

Fully Present

While David set his heart to seek the one thing, Jesus later required this same focus when He was welcomed into the home of Mary and Martha:

> As Jesus and his disciples were on their way, he came to a village where a woman named Martha opened her home to him. She had a sister called Mary, who sat at the Lord's feet listening to what he said. But Martha was distracted by all the preparations that had to be made. She came to him and asked, "Lord, don't you care that my sister has left me to do the work by myself? Tell her to help me!"
>
> "Martha, Martha," the Lord answered, "you are worried and upset about many things, but only *one thing* is needed. Mary has chosen what is better, and it will not be taken away from her."
>
> Luke 10:38–42, emphasis mine

"Only one thing is needed," Jesus said—to sit at His feet. The hardest battle for most to fight is not necessarily choosing the good over the bad; it is choosing the best over the good when two honorable options are presented. Mary chose the better when she put aside all other endeavors to remain absorbed in Jesus when He was present. Martha did a noble thing by desiring to serve Him. Jesus did not want to be served in that moment, however; He wanted to be in relationship with her. Serving Him became a distraction to encountering Him.

It is important to know when it is time to serve and when it is time to let everything go and simply be present. There will be moments of resting in His presence and also times to step out and act.[3] There is nothing wrong with Martha wanting to honor Jesus by serving Him well. But in this particular instance, the better way was to sit at Jesus' feet, as Mary chose to do. The one thing that was most important to Jesus in that moment was being together and enjoying each other's presence.

When Jesus is present, He wants us to let other things go. Ministry, planning, details, schedules and preparations can be put to the side when He walks into the room. When He draws near, He deserves our full attention. If we are fully present with God, He will be fully present with us.

Azusa

In the early days of the Azusa Street revival in 1906, people gathered for one purpose, to seek more of God.[4] Their only agenda was to encounter Him. Eyewitness and historian of the revival, Frank Bartleman, said that in the meetings "there was no closing at 9 o'clock sharp, as the preachers must do today in order to keep the people. We wanted God in those days. We did not have a thousand other things we wanted before Him."[5] In their generation, they had to fight off "a thousand other things" that might steal their focus from Jesus. In our current generation, we have so many more distractions and options to choose from that we need to say no to "a million other things" in order to say yes to Jesus.

I wonder what it looks like not to have "a thousand other things" we want before God? When everything is stripped away, it is easy to see that all we have is Jesus. But what do we do when the excess of life surrounds us and competes for first place? What do we do when we have a million other options and images competing for our attention, calling out to us, "Choose me, pick me!" Where, what and to whom do we run when the storms infiltrate our minds, hearts and lives? Is Jesus still all we have when we have a million other options we can also run to? Is Jesus still worth putting ourselves into greater danger just to be with Him? What kind of increased revival fire would be present in a generation that says no to a million things to say the one yes to the one thing? What would it look like if Jesus were our one and only focus today?

Inspired Focus

Missionary Lilias Trotter lived a focused life. While she was living in Africa with an unreached people group, her own life intertwined in their culture and daily life, she wrote a short story and song that would later inspire Helen H. Lemmel to pen the worship song "Turn Your Eyes upon Jesus" in 1922. Prepare your heart to receive this powerful impartation from Lilias Trotter.

Focussed: A Story and a Song

It was in a little wood in early morning. The sun was climbing behind a steep cliff in the east, and its light was flooding nearer and nearer and then making pools among the trees. Suddenly, from a dark corner of purple brown stems and tawny moss, there shone out a great golden star. It was just a dandelion, and half withered—but it was full face to the sun, and had caught into its heart all the glory it could hold, and was shining so radiantly that the dew that lay on it still made a perfect aureole round its head. And it seemed to talk, standing there—to talk about the possibility of making the very best of these lives of ours.

For if the Sun of Righteousness has risen upon our hearts, there is an ocean of grace and love and power lying all around us, an ocean to which all earthly light is but a drop, and it is ready to transfigure us, as the sunshine transfigured the dandelion, and on the same condition—that we stand full face to God.

Gathered up, focussed lives, intent on one aim—Christ— these are the lives on which God can concentrate blessedness. It is "all for all" by a law as unvarying as any law that governs the material universe.

We see the principle shadowed in the trend of science; the telephone and the wireless in the realm of sound, the use of radium and the ultra violet rays in the realm of light. All these work by gathering into focus currents and waves that, dispersed, cannot serve us. In every branch of learning and workmanship the tendency of these days is to specialize—to take up one point and follow it to the uttermost.

And Satan knows well the power of concentration, if a soul is likely to get under the sway of the inspiration, "this one thing I do," he will turn all his energies to bring in side-interests that will shatter the gathering intensity.

And they lie all around, these interests. Never has it been so easy to live in half a dozen good harmless worlds at once— art, music, social science, games, motoring, the following of some profession, and so on. And between them we run the risk of drifting about, the "good" hiding the "best" even more effectually than it could be hidden by downright frivolity with its smothered heart-ache at its own emptiness.

It is easy to find out whether our lives are focused, and if so, where the focus lies. Where do our thoughts settle when consciousness comes back in the morning? Where do they swing back when the pressure is off during the day? Does this test not give the clue? Then dare to have it out with God— and after all, that is the shortest way. Dare to lay bare your whole life and being before Him, and ask Him to show you whether or not all is focussed on Christ and His glory. Dare to face the fact that unfocussed good and useful as it may seem, it will prove to have failed of its purpose.

What does this focussing mean? Study the matter and you will see that it means two things—gathering in all that can be gathered, and letting the rest drop. The working of any lens—microscope, telescope, camera—will show you this. The lens of your own eye, in the room where you are sitting, as clearly as any other. Look at the window bars, and the beyond is only a shadow; look through at the distance, and it is the bars that turn into ghosts. You have to choose which you will fix your gaze upon and let the other go.

Are we ready for a cleavage to be wrought through the whole range of our lives, like the division long ago at the taking of Jericho, the division between things that could be passed through the fire of consecration into "the treasury of the Lord," and the things that, unable to "bide the fire," must be destroyed? All aims, all ambitions, all desires, all pursuits—shall we dare to drop them if they cannot be gathered sharply and clearly into the focus of "this one thing I do"?

Will it not make life narrow, this focusing? In a sense, it will—just as the mountain path grows narrower, for it matters more and more, the higher we go, where we set our feet—but there is always, as it narrows, a wider and wider outlook and purer, clearer air. Narrow as Christ's life was narrow, this is our aim; narrow as regards self-seeking, broad as the love of God to all around. Is there anything to fear in that?

And in the narrowing and focussing, the channel will be prepared for God's power—like the stream hemmed between the rockbeds, that wells up in a spring—like the burning glass that gathers the rays into an intensity that will kindle fire. It is worth while to let God see what He can do with these lives of ours, when "to live is Christ."

How do we bring things to a focus in the world of optics? Not by looking at the things to be dropped, but by looking at the one point that is to be brought out.

Turn full your soul's vision to Jesus, and look and look at Him, and a strange dimness will come over all that is apart from Him, and the Divine "attrait" by which God's saints are made, even in this 20th century, will lay hold of you. For "He is worthy" to have all there is to be had in the heart that He has died to win.[6]

Regaining Focus through Silence

Turning our eyes upon Jesus and focusing on His face is one of the most fruitful endeavors we can pursue. Psalm 46:10 says, "Be still, and know that I am God." Being still in un-interrupted silence is a great way to regain focus on Jesus as well as to let all distractions disappear from our lives. When we lean in to listen to His voice, we can better mute all the voices outside.

I often begin preaching with extended periods of silence to focus on Jesus. It helps me settle on hearing His heart, being in His presence and waiting for His anointing to rest upon me. It also makes people feel very uncomfortable at times because God is beginning to remove hindrances to His incoming presence. Time after time, as we focus on Jesus and invite the Holy Spirit to come, God's presence invades the room in a way that can only be described as a purifying fire. His weighty presence falls, and people one after another begin to weep in the room. They have finally stilled their lives long enough to let the true and deep issues of the heart begin to emerge in the context of the Father's love. He comes in the midst of their pain and begins to heal them right then and there, many times without anyone even laying hands on them to pray for them. Still other times, in silence and in keeping our eyes on Him, people hear from the Lord again, get creative ideas or even get solutions to their problems.

There is something about the simplicity of silence and being focused on His presence that brings people out of the clutter of life back to the one thing.

ACTIVATION: Be Still and Know

Spend five to fifteen (or more) minutes in silence each day this week, focusing on the face of Jesus and being absorbed in His presence. Use Psalm 27 as your text if you want to include a reading. Invite the Holy Spirit to come and rest upon you. Welcome the fire of God to come and burn away anything that would distract you. Spend time listening to His heart. Enjoy this journey and give yourself tons of grace. Silence and waiting on God is a lost art and hard to do at first, but with practice it gets easier.[7] Your only goal here is to be with Jesus and to behold His beauty, not to pray or to get breakthrough or anything else. Journal afterward (not during) about how it was for you, what you felt and what God showed you during that time.

As you set aside time to simply love on Jesus with no other agenda, I pray that face-to-face encounters are released. I pray for great grace on your life as you embrace the gift of silence. May the fire of God fall on you and burn away anything holding you back from being fully absorbed in His presence. May the love of God compel you to turn your eyes upon Jesus always.

7

Full Attention

We just discovered the significance of keeping our eyes on Jesus and how the lost art of silence is a grace that can act as a refining fire to help regain focus. In this chapter, we will discover the impact of focus, why the enemy wants to sidetrack us from Jesus and from each other, and how to remove distractions to help position us to be more present with Jesus and with those around us.

Distracted

"Then Peter got down out of the boat, walked on the water and came toward Jesus. But when he saw the wind, he was afraid and, beginning to sink, cried out, 'Lord, save me!'" (Matthew 14:29–30).

No sooner had Peter taken his eyes off Jesus than he began to sink and cease doing the impossible. He allowed the fear of the storm to supersede his gaze. Not only that, but Peter put his focus on something that cannot be seen. We cannot actually see wind; we can only see its impact all around us. The wind stirred up a storm, which competed for Peter's attention and distracted him from the one thing. He took his focus off Jesus, who is the Truth, and put it on a lie that his circumstances had more power than Jesus.

There seems to be an assault on our generation trying to keep our focus away from Jesus. Too many distractions, options, images and other lovers compete for our adoration that is intended to be for Jesus alone. False love replaces our deepest desires to connect with the God of the universe and with each other. One of the reasons why the enemy is so adamant about distracting us is because when our focus remains on Him, we end up doing the impossible, like Peter did. Our hearts become impenetrable because we become one with God. I believe God is drawing this generation to a more intense gaze than we have known before.

Social Media Fast

In the summer of 2016, I decided to go on a social media fast. I wanted to unplug, reset and begin dreaming about what God had for me in the upcoming season, without distraction. I wanted to go back to my mystic roots and become a minimalist once again. Silence is one of my love languages; I love to sit at the lake for hours and just think. With social media in my life, however, I was regularly torn between the beauty in front of me and the false sense of connection I felt by looking down at my phone. I wanted my thoughts to be pure, refined and deeper than what social media required of me. I was also getting ready to dive into writing this book. I reflected on what it must have been like for someone like Madame Jeanne Guyon or Jane Austen to write a book—long days with lots of silence, quiet space and time to think deep thoughts. I wanted the book to come from a deep well, not something fragmented, impulsive, shallow or flashy. I felt that there might be a hidden place in my heart I could explore more fully. I knew that to get to the depths of that journey inward, I would need to be unhindered by distractions.

I confess that before the fast I had been checking social media regularly throughout each day and even into the evening in excessive measures. Instant gratification, immediate response time and scanning other people's news feeds contributed to making me more impulsive than ever. My addiction to social media began to change even the way I thought, causing me to think shorter thoughts. Rather than having deep conversations and connecting with people in real time, I was often distracted, wanting to check my accounts. I could not sit still anymore without this obsession drawing me to "engage" with the virtual world. I was on a roller coaster that I could not get off of.

Dr. Caroline Leaf, Ph.D., who has worked in the area of cognitive neuroscience, wrote a book called *Switch on Your Brain* (2013). Through her research she shows that multitasking, especially as it relates to social media, results in greater levels of stress, depression, rash thinking and impulsive decision making. It also results in greater impulse buying, credit card debt and overeating. Using social media has become as addicting as alcohol and drug abuse.[1]

The problem was that my addiction to social media owned me instead of serving purposes that would align with my values. While sitting with Jesus at the lake one morning, I felt the sudden urge to deactivate my social media accounts so I could completely break this addiction and regain unhindered focus on His face. I did not realize that doing such a small act would be so countercultural and revolutionary in my personal life.

The first week after coming off social media, I had withdrawals. The fast made me realize that every time I woke up, was stressed out, went to the bathroom, got away from the crowds—or even when I was with people—I had a compulsion to check my accounts, even if just out of habit. I had not realized how much of my life had been given over to this addiction. During the fast, I had to learn how to restructure my thinking. I was living life and enjoying the moment, but how would I share these experiences with my friends? Where would I post pictures of my epic surfing adventures in Bali or of my new baby nephew whom I met for the first time in Thailand? Rather than posting a picture for the masses, I had to redefine how and with whom I would share these experiences. The fast helped me to redefine and focus. It made me be more intentional with those I wanted to do life with and those I wanted to invite deeper into my heart.

Free from Addiction

One thing I learned on this fast was that it was very liberating not to have to check my account every five minutes after I posted something to see who liked it or had commented. It was wonderful being able to be fully present in the conversation with the person in front of me rather than checking to see which of my thousands of "friends," who were not present in that moment, responded to one of my posts.

During the fast, I enjoyed a simpler and more focused life. I journaled more often, spent more time outside enjoying the summer with friends, climbed mountains and had deeper conversations without being distracted. I connected with friends from around the world with whom I had not connected for more than a year. I read more books, spent more time with family and let my heart feel at a deeper level. I deep cleaned and purged my house and, it seemed, my life. I got more focused on the Lord and prayed more often. I learned to grow in vulnerability, be uncomfortable and remain with the people I was with instead of escaping to my phone all of the time.

This fast also helped me set good boundaries for social media upon my return so that I could limit myself from the constant infiltration of words, videos and pictures of others' lives and begin to live my life more fully in the moment. I wanted my relationship with social media to be life-giving to myself and to all of my "friends." Social media has the potential to be a wonderful tool for releasing the power of the testimony, inspiring others and sharing my heart with the world. I wanted to make sure that when I came back to it, I was purposeful and utilized social media as a blessing rather than allowing it to take over my life.

I discovered that life is too short to waste it looking down all the time. Removing distractions in my life during that season helped me to focus and redefine the direction I was to take next. There is something beautiful about positioning oneself to let God strip away every distraction in order to see Him more. Once the addiction was broken, I needed to replace it with something life-giving. Reading books, memorizing Scripture and being intentional with others were great places to start. Worshiping was one of the best ways for me to focus and fully engage with God. Playing the piano and even praying with others helped keep me accountable to remain in His presence. Overall, I experienced a great deal of freedom and peace as a result of the fast, and I grew in the ability to be fully present with people.

The Matrix

In the process of reflecting on my personal journey in the midst of my social media fast, I was reminded of the movie *The Matrix* (1999). The longer I had been off social media, the freer I felt and the more I realized how enslaved I had been. It felt to me almost like the scene in *The Matrix* when Neo was offered the choice between the red pill or the blue pill. The blue pill would keep things as they were so he could continue in mere existence, numb to the reality behind his life. The red pill would wake him up, literally opening his eyes to what was really going on in a society that had yet to awaken to who they really were.

On this fast, I felt like I took the "red pill." I became free from my own addiction and began to live life again in the present. Unattached to my phone and set free from the impulsive urge for immediate gratification, I began to notice how many others were entrapped under the illusion that this type of shallow connection could replace the true, deep heart connection we were born for. When I was out in public, I was surprised to see how many people were tied to their mobile devices. Countless times at dinner with a friend, I noticed people around us sitting in front of each other at the table but focusing on their phones rather than engaging in live conversation.

If we really did have a chance to sit down with Jesus for a one-on-one chat over coffee, I wonder how many of us would be able to drop everything and be fully present. Would the nagging compulsion to check our social media accounts pull our attention away from the One sitting in front of us? How long could we simply sit with Jesus before we felt the urge to check our phones?

Why the Assault?

As we read in 1 Timothy 6:10, money in and of itself is not the source of all evil—the love of money is. Money can, in fact, be a great resource for advancing God's Kingdom. In the same way, social media or the excess of options is not really our enemy. The enemy uses even potentially good things to distract us from God's purposes. An assault has been released against our generation to steal our focus. We must be aware that the enemy has a plan and that he is using distractions and the busyness in our lives to take our focus off Jesus.

As I continued to ponder this assault against our generation and the war to keep hearts and minds distracted from the one thing, I began to ask the question, *Why?* Why would the enemy try to get us wrapped up in being disconnected, isolated and distracted? What great things is God about to do in our midst that require unity, connection, alignment and focus? What would happen if people were present with each other once more?

Distractions keep us from focusing on the one thing and isolate us from each other. They can also keep us from assembling and aligning our lives to bring light into the darkest of places. Focusing on Jesus helps usher in the fire of God to bring light in the night seasons. There is something powerful in focus and connection. When a group of people can focus and work together on what God has called them to release, it changes lives and can impact generations.

I believe that God is raising up a new breed of revolutionaries who will say no to the seductions of the world and who will live counterculturally. He is calling us to go deeper with Him and with each other. He has divine strategies and purposes for each one that are hidden in the depths of His heart and within each other. The only way to access these is to go deep with Him and with one another. This requires quality time, vulnerability and being present without distractions.

There are deeper places in our hearts God wants to journey into if we let Him. This requires removing all distractions to be fully present with Him. It means being uncomfortable and sitting through the awkward silence. There will be times when we do not feel anything, and we will want to run away and retreat to the busyness and stimulation we get by checking our phones and devices. We need simply to be still and remain in Him. We need to continue to fight for deep and real connection with others. It will be well worth the fight, I promise you.

ACTIVATION: **Being Fully Present**

We already began to cultivate inner silence and communion with God in the previous chapter. Now I want to ask: When was the last time you were truly present with the person in front of you?

Below are a few suggestions to help you grow in being fully present, not only with God but also with the people around you.

1. Go out to dinner or coffee with a friend and leave your phone behind. Try to maintain eye contact longer than you have before. Listen more and seek to really understand the other person's heart. Speak a word of encouragement and share why that friend is important to you. Be more vulnerable with that friend than you have in the past.

2. Take a week off from your social media accounts or any other addiction God has revealed to you while reading this chapter. The purpose of fasting from food, social media or anything else is so that we can better feast on Jesus. Dr. Leaf also explains in *Switch on Your Brain* how we can train and rewire our brains through our

minds by what we think and choose to meditate on. She writes that what we intentionally focus on can shape our brains, hearts, bodies, attitudes and actions. Keeping our focus on Jesus and meditating on His promises has actually proved to bring greater levels of health and happiness.[2]

In light of these findings, every time you have the urge to check your accounts, instead read some favorite Bible verses, pray for someone or sing a worship song. Begin to feed your soul and spirit in a new way. During this experiment, how often did you find yourself checking your phone or other device? What changes in your life did you make this week? What did you learn about yourself? What boundaries do you want to set for yourself if or when you return to social media? What will be your renewed purpose in investing time in social media upon your return?

Journal your answers and submit to the Lord any heart issues that have emerged. Continue to ask for His refining fire to come and purify you and give you an undivided heart.

8

Forward Momentum

As long as Peter kept his eyes fixed on Jesus and moved in forward momentum toward Him, he continued to do the impossible. Moving closer to Jesus every chance we get will help us fulfill our destiny and will also act as a safeguard to protect us from sinking.

We are always moving; the question is in which direction. When the Israelites were presented with the opportunity to inherit the Promised Land, instead of choosing courage, they embraced fear. Instead of moving toward the abundance God had awaiting them, they wanted to go backward into the land of their bondage. They were even willing to forfeit the ground they had already gained to do so (see Numbers 14).[1]

When we are presented with a choice, forward momentum is not only crucial to stepping into the impossible; it is a life-or-death matter that holds our destiny in the balance. There is no middle ground. Apathy is a killer. Remaining stationary or standing still when an invitation to come closer beckons means one can easily be seduced into deeper darkness than before. King Hezekiah trusted in the Lord, held fast to Him and "did not cease to follow Him." Because of this forward momentum and continual pursuit of God, "the LORD was with him [and] he was successful in whatever he undertook" (2 Kings 18:5–7). By always choosing to keep our eyes on Jesus and walk toward Him, we protect ourselves from fulfilling the lust of the flesh. Once we get distracted, hesitate, stop or lose focus by putting our attention on the storm around us rather than on Him, we begin to sink. It is imperative to continue moving toward Jesus in all circumstances. If we do this, we will remain safe in Him, fulfill our God-given destinies and go from glory to glory.

Do you realize that in the passage describing the armor of God in Ephesians 6:10–17, there is no armor protecting one's back? We conquer the enemy by moving forward, on the offensive. If we turn back to where we just came from, we are unprotected. The safest place to be is exactly where God is leading us, no matter if that is in a war zone, in some far-off country or in the middle of the sea. Forward momentum protects us from sinking in the storms and enables us to partner with God for the impossible.

Walk in the Spirit

The word translated "walk" used in Matthew 14:29, when Peter walked on water, is the Greek word *peripateo*. It means how people conduct their lives or how they live. By walking on water, Peter literally stepped into the same authority and dominion over the laws of nature as Jesus. When we walk in the footsteps of Jesus, we accept His invitation to live an empowered life. Galatians 5:16 also makes clear that when we walk in the Spirit, we will not fulfill the lust of the flesh.

When we are full of Jesus and His Spirit, we will not have an empty void to try to fill with other things.

Walking in the Spirit, keeping our eyes on Jesus and fulfilling the assignments God has called us to (see Ephesians 2:10) are crucial to embracing the abundant life and keeping us away from sin. King David experienced this the hard way when he chose not to engage in his assignment during a particular season. "In the spring, at the time when kings go off to war, David sent Joab out with the king's men and the whole Israelite army. They destroyed the Ammonites and besieged Rabbah. But David remained in Jerusalem" (2 Samuel 11:1). By not engaging in the battle he was born for, King David got bored and was left with plenty of time to let his mind wander to other things. He eventually committed adultery with Bathsheba and later had her husband killed. If he had been in war during the time when kings go to war, he would never have found himself in that place of temptation. By not stepping into the forward momentum of his destiny, David fulfilled the lust of the flesh.

I remember a season in my life during my midtwenties when I was not going after the Lord or my calling wholeheartedly. I knew deep down I was born to preach. I had even received many prophetic words about this, but God was not opening those doors at that time in my life, and I was not sure what to do or where to go next. I let disappointment sink in. I pretty much gave up on my dream to preach and instead began to live a "normal" life. I shifted from believing the truth that I was called to bring revival and instead moved into the place of discouragement because it was not happening in my timeline.

During this darker season, I stopped discipling women, which I knew I was born for. I also stopped pursuing Jesus in the hard places, where taking risks to find Him would be uncomfortable. I struggled to invite Him into the vulnerable places in my heart and found myself sinking in a storm of disappointment, doubt and confusion.

Since I was no longer seeking Jesus wholeheartedly, intentionally walking in the Spirit or moving forward toward my destiny, I began to make poor choices. One small decision after another caused my heart to decay. For an individual who felt destined to be a consecrated one and to carry revival to the nations, these small decisions could easily have grown into a deeper, destructive lifestyle of compromise or sin. I had given up on my dreams and allowed things of the world to fill the void. I still walked with God somewhat, but I had stopped burning for Him the way I knew I was born to do.

I think we have all had seasons like that, when things are not working out the way we hoped or imagined. Sometimes we yield to the world's temptations to give up and conform. But there is something powerful in turning our eyes back upon the face of Jesus and leaning in toward Him that makes everything right. We are called to persevere. He wants to take us to the place where our eyes never leave His and where we are inspired to move toward Him always.

Run with Perseverance

Beyond simply walking in the Spirit, God is also calling us to *run* the race set before us with perseverance, keeping our eyes fixed on Jesus. Hebrews 12:1–3 says,

> Therefore, since we are surrounded by such a great cloud of witnesses, let us throw off everything that hinders and the sin that so easily entangles, and let us run with perseverance the race marked out for us. Let us fix our eyes on Jesus, the author and perfecter of our faith, who for the joy set before

him endured the cross, scorning its shame, and sat down at the right hand of the throne of God. Consider him who endured such opposition from sinful men, so that you will not grow weary and lose heart.

When we are running wholeheartedly toward Jesus and the calling of God He has placed on our lives, we are safe in the midst of the storms and empowered to do the impossible. This focus on Jesus and on a consecrated lifestyle accelerates us into our destiny. We gain even more momentum when we strip off the things that weigh us down.

We move faster and farther if we carry less. Everything we are carrying in this season should be what God has laid there for us. Just because we did something in one season that brought us life does not mean that it will be life-giving in the next. With all the options of where to spend our time and which relationships to invest in, it is important to discern which season we are in and to align our lives, schedules and relationships accordingly, so that we are able to steward God's call for our lives well. Sometimes what God has anointed in one season will not continue into the next.

While I was writing this book, I had lots of other great opportunities available to me. One of these was to continue teaching at my church's ministry school, something I felt born for. When I considered my upcoming schedule with all of these wonderful and good options, I felt overwhelmed and stressed out, and I was losing focus on everything and everyone that was in front of me. All of the opportunities were good, but I knew that I could not carry each of them with excellence in the same season. Good is usually the enemy of best. I had to discern which things were the gold that God had put in my life at that time and which were silver. Just because some of them might have been silver then did not mean that they would not turn into gold at a different time.

I struggled with some hard decisions. I remember talking with a spiritual father, Mark Brookes, who helps run the ministry school. He, too, recognized that I could not do everything with excellence and that something would have to give. I had to lay down my dream of teaching at the ministry school the first half of the year so I could focus and better steward the other things I felt God had highlighted. I even canceled a ministry trip and one of my Writing in the Glory workshops, which I had never done before. Once I let those things go, I instantly felt peace. I was able to focus on the relationships in front of me and run wholeheartedly toward what I felt God had prioritized in my life for that season.

Sometimes we need to let go of things in our lives that are good but that we do not have peace about at that time. Evan Roberts, who pioneered the Welsh revival of 1904–1905, believed that for genuine revival to take place, anything that gave place to doubt about whether it was good or evil needed to be removed. Each night in the early revival services, he shared these four ways of living:

1. We must confess before God every sin in our past lives that has not been confessed.
2. We must remove anything that is doubtful in our lives.
3. Total surrender—we must say and do all that the Spirit tells us.
4. We must make a public confession of Christ.[2]

If there are any commitments or relationships in your life that you have doubted for some time, it might be a good idea to explore with the Holy Spirit why that is and if the Lord is asking you to surrender them afresh to Him. Letting go of the good to embrace the best will increase your forward momentum toward the things Jesus is calling you to step into. It would be unwise to attempt to walk on water carrying extra weight that might cause you to sink.

ACTIVATION: **Positioning Yourself to Run the Race**

1. Write out your life vision or purpose statement. What were you born to do? What kind of impact do you feel you are called to make?

2. Write out your present commitments in this season.

    Which of these commitments support your life vision and calling?

    Which commitments might be good but do not support or align with your destiny?

    Of these, which can you completely let go of and which need to be passed on to someone else?

    Is there anyone else who can take responsibility for anything in your life that is not yours to carry right now?

    I encourage you to do whatever is necessary to make sure that everything you are committing to in this season contributes to your life vision and destiny so that you can be walking in the Spirit to the fullest measure. There are countless great causes you can be a part of today, but there is one specific cause that only you were born to carry. Do not let participation in the great causes distract you from investing in the one cause you would be willing to lay down your life for.

3. Think of one word or theme that you are most passionate about right now that the Holy Spirit is burning inside

of you to go after (healing, family, revival, intimacy, evangelism, etc.).

Now think of others in your life who are passionate about this same thing. Ask the Holy Spirit to highlight four mentors, four peers and four people to disciple in this season who also burn for the thing that you burn for right now.

Mentors/spiritual mothers and fathers:

1.

2.

3.

4.

Friends/peers:

1.

2.

3.

4.

People to mentor/disciple:

1.

2.

3.

4.

This is a clarifying activity to help you prioritize, focus and invest your time wisely into those the Holy Spirit is highlighting. This list will change in different seasons of life. Just because a friend is not passionate about the same thing you are right now does not mean that friend is not just as important in your life as before.

Make time for the people who matter to you even if they do not share the same passion; do, however, also try to look for those who burn for what you do, so that you can strategically run together after the things of God. Once you have your list of twelve people whom the Holy Spirit has highlighted for you, try to be more intentional in sharing your heart and prioritizing time with these in this season. Then watch and see what fruit will come.

4. I encourage you to declare this prayer out loud and see how God wants to meet you in this moment. Let the fire come. . . .

> Holy Spirit, I invite Your fire to fall over all of my relationships, commitments, desires and affections. Come and align my life according to Your perfect will. I give You permission to rearrange my life, my priorities and my schedule in whatever way will help me to better focus on Your face. Burn away anything in my life that is not what You want for me in this season. Give me wisdom to discern the good from the best. I welcome Your refining fire to purify the gold and melt away the excess. Strip off anything that would easily entangle me so that I can run full speed ahead toward Your loving face. Anything that is hard for me to let go of, I give You full permission to take away today. I put all of my trust in You. Let me be so undone by Your love that nothing else matters than running after You with my whole heart. Be the only One who can pull on my heartstrings today. You have my ultimate yes. I choose to run after You with everything inside of me, nothing holding me back.

9

It Was Not Jesus' Idea

Did you notice that it was not Jesus' idea for Peter to walk on water? "'Lord, if it's you,' Peter replied, 'tell me to come to you on the water'" (Matthew 14:28). It was Peter who suggested doing the impossible alongside Jesus. He wanted to be closer to Jesus, and if that meant defying the laws of nature to do so, nothing was going to hold him back. Peter's boldness in following his heart and his vulnerability in risk taking opened the way for him to do the impossible. And Jesus backed up his request. It is crucial we learn from Peter's example and readily live from our hearts like he did in that moment.

Purifying Our Desires in His Presence

As we spend time in God's presence, He molds and shapes the desires of our hearts to be in tune with His. His desires begin to become our own. The psalmist said, "Delight yourself in the LORD and he will give you the desires of your heart"

(Psalm 37:4). If we are faithful to steward our relationships with the Lord and to enjoy Him, He will grant us our hearts' pure desires. Feasting on God by dwelling in His presence transforms our thoughts, hopes and desires to be in alignment with His. As we delight in Him, He shapes our desires. Then when we ask Him to give us the desires of our hearts, He knows that He can trust us with those dreams because we have spent the time getting to know His heart. We can also pursue the passions in our hearts knowing that we are in union with the Lord. As we saturate our lives in His presence, He waters and grows those seeds of destiny (Isaiah 61:11).

Rather than waiting around for God to tell us what to do all of the time, we can also recognize times in our lives when He wants us to pursue the desires of our hearts. Psalm 20:4 says, "May he give you the desire of your heart and make all your plans succeed." The Scripture says in both this verse and Psalm 37:4, may He give *you* the desires of *your* heart. There are unique desires in each of us that are sourced in Him. These look different for each person. We live in relationship with Him in which we are given free will and can explore and discover what makes our hearts come alive. The more we spend time communing with God, the more we can begin to trust that our desires are in line with His heart.

A monk named Thomas Merton once said, "A tree glorifies God by being a tree." This means that I can glorify God by simply being my unique and awesome self. I am irreplaceable. I have certain passions and desires that are unique to me because of how I was intricately woven together in my mother's womb by the hand of God (Psalm 139:13). There are some activities that make me come alive and others I do not enjoy at all. I am passionate about surfing and being in or near the water. I feel the pleasure of God when I am in water. On the contrary, I do not really enjoy long periods of being in the snow or cold, although some people love that. It is okay if I am different from others; that is how I am wired. I am specifically handcrafted by the Creator of the universe. I was born to ride waves and to display His glory through every part of my life. I shine for Him best when I am most fully alive. If I embrace who God has made me to be without wasting my time trying to be someone else, He receives glory. By being fully me, another facet of God is revealed to the world in the way He expresses Himself through my life.

It is also important to realize that God actually trusts us. If we have spent time developing our relationship with Him and learning His heart, we can know that our desires will be pure. Jesus said, "If you remain in me and my words remain in you, ask whatever you wish, and it will be given you" (John 15:7). These are not selfish desires for greedy gain that we are asking to be fulfilled. These are desires for the abundant life that Jesus died for us to have. These are all the things we need to fulfill the call of God on our lives. These are even desires to bless those around us.

He wants to give you the desires of *your* heart. A father loves to bless his children specifically with what will make them happy, and our heavenly Father is the original father, who models that love for us. As long as we abide in the love of the Father, we can learn to trust our hearts and live from a place of total freedom to be fully ourselves.

God's Masterpiece

"For we are God's workmanship, created in Christ Jesus to do good works, which God prepared in advance for us to do" (Ephesians 2:10).

We are God's masterpiece, His poem written to the world to display more of His glory. He has already gone ahead of us and prepared works beforehand for us to walk in. If you are passionate about something or have great dreams for the future, it is because God planted those ideas and desires in your heart long ago.

I remember a time when Ephesians 2:10 became very real to me. In 2006, while I was a manager and trainer for Starbucks, I had the opportunity to go to a leadership training class. For one of our activities, we were asked to write out a list of goals and dreams. One of the goals I wrote was that I wanted to "write a book about revolutionaries/revivals." Years later, during the summer of 2012, the Holy Spirit opened the door for me to work on a book project with Bill Johnson, the pastor of Bethel Church in Redding, California. This started as a summer job, to help him do research for a book about defining moments of revival leaders; it later developed into a multiyear project, for which I actually got paid to help write a book with one of my heroes of the faith. *Defining Moments* came out in January 2016, ten years after I had first had the inspired idea to write it. It astonishes me how good God is and how He fulfills the specific and unique desires of our hearts.

In 1 Samuel 1–2, Hannah had a deep and passionate desire in her heart to have a son. She desperately wanted a child. She entreated God to hear her prayer and to give her the desire of her heart. While Hannah wanted a son, God also wanted a prophet to save Israel. Her desire was the same as God's dream for the nation. My dream to write a book about revivals was the same dream God put into Bill's heart years later, and then He divinely intersected us. God's dream was not only for me to be sustained during a challenging season of planting Destiny House, but also that through the book many people would be led into life-changing encounters with God.

Martin Luther King Jr. had a dream that affected a nation and changed history. Many times when God puts a desire in our hearts, it is not just about us fulfilling a dream. Most of the time our dream is tied to someone else's destiny. For us to live our dreams means that others will be empowered, healed, set free and significantly impacted. Our dreams are not to be taken lightly or to be thrown whimsically to the side because we feel they are too outlandish or that they are just our own thoughts. God has uniquely wired each one of us and is waiting for us to fulfill the specific dreams He has placed inside of us. People's lives are depending upon our saying yes to following our hearts.

Water to Wine

Peter was present for Jesus' very first miracle, when He turned water into wine (John 2). Jesus, His mother and His disciples had all been invited to a wedding party. During the party, the wine ran out, which could have been a great embarrassment for the groom. Jesus told the servants to fill six water pots full of water, which He later turned into wine. While the servants were told what to do and also witnessed the miracle, the bridegroom was unaware of what had happened at his own party. Jesus did a miracle behind the scenes on his behalf as he simply followed his heart to covenant with the woman he was promised to. The best thing the groom did besides follow his heart was to invite Jesus to the party.

I love this story, because I believe God wants to make a massive shift in our generation from what is embedded in this narrative. We can remain servants of the Lord, wait around to hear His audible voice and then do exactly what He says. This is good, and it allowed these servants to partner with Jesus and actually see the miracle. But I feel that God is leading our generation into a new level of relationship with Jesus. God wants us to follow our hearts and invite Jesus to the party. He wants friendship and partnership with us and to co-labor with us. He is waiting for us to follow our hearts because He wants to surprise us, bless us and back us up in incredible ways, just like He did for Peter walking on water.

Drive-Through Money

I love to bodyboard, surf and be at the beach. It makes me come alive inside. One winter, when I spent Christmas with my family in Orange County, God did a unique sign as I followed my heart to go to the beach. On December 30, 2015, I woke up early and checked out the surf report online to see if there were any waves. Usually I wake up around six in the morning to head to the beach before it gets crowded. This time, however, I hesitated and struggled to get out of my nice, cozy, warm bed. Then, around a quarter past nine, I made up my mind that I was going to get in one last surf session before I flew back to Northern California. This was three hours after my usual time of heading to the beach.

I finally jumped in the car and was on my way. As I approached an intersection about a mile away from my parents' home, I noticed something unusual in the street. Just ahead of me papers were swirling in the air above the road. I was not sure what was going on, but when I got closer, I saw what looked like twenty-dollar bills floating in the wind from passing cars. I said to myself, *This cannot be right. It has to be fake money, or it must belong to someone.* I nearly kept driving, but my curiosity got the best of me. I quickly turned left into a restaurant parking lot and ventured into the center divide of the street, where another guy was grabbing as many bills as possible.

I asked him if he knew whose money it was, but he said he did not. I wondered if this was drug money God was reclaiming back into the Kingdom. Nobody knew whose money it was, and no one was there to claim it. Once I got it cleared up that we could not find the owner, it felt like being in a movie. I literally started grabbing the money from the air and on the ground. After waiting for cars to pass, I and the few others also there walked back out onto the street to pick up twenty-dollar bill after twenty-dollar bill. We were not even competing with each other to get more money. We were so elated, like children in a candy store, that we pointed them out to each other, calling out, "Hey, there's one over there—grab it!" One lady on the other side of the street gathered $360, and I later found out it was her birthday. Wow! What a way to be celebrated!

It blew me away. Within only a few minutes, all of the money had been picked up by the few of us who had stopped when we saw something unusual in the street. If I had decided to go to the beach at the normal time, I never would have driven through all of this money. If I had not turned aside to see what was going on, I would have missed out. I ended up gathering $240 that day before getting back into my car and continuing on to the beach for my last surf session of the year! When I returned home, I was able to use that money to pay off a debt I owed my mom, which enabled me to enter the new year free from that obligation.

This experience made me realize that God can literally make money appear out of thin air. I was marked by the truth that the lack of money can never be an excuse in my life for not stepping out in faith in the direction God is leading. I had just been minding my own business and going on an adventure to the beach. I was not doing anything spiritual at all. I could not have avoided this unique blessing if I had wanted to; I literally was forced to drive right through the money at precisely the right time. If I had left five minutes before or after, I would have missed the moment. I am glad I decided to follow my heart to go to the beach one last time, and I am thankful that I recognized something was happening and turned aside.

This sign is always a reminder to me that there are times that I cannot escape God's blessings even if I tried. Sometimes when we are paying attention the least, God wants to apprehend and surprise us with His goodness. Sometimes as we follow our hearts, we intersect the impossible without mustering up any faith at all. Sometimes the impossible has nothing to do with faith, but everything to do with Him showing us His goodness. Other times it comes when we simply follow the desires of our hearts to enjoy Him and to live the abundant life He died for us to have, even if that means going to spend a day at the beach.

Running on Water

In the summer of 2014, a South African friend named Matthew Shutte, who lived at Destiny House along with his wife, Lisa, gave me a powerful prophetic word during one of our family nights together. In the prophetic picture, he saw me as a white horse in a stable. Jesus was there, brushing and grooming me like His prized possession. After this, He took me by a rope and led me to a beach. This beach ran for eternity; there was no end to it. A small strip of land ran parallel to the ocean.

The Lord took me by the reins, let go and told me to run. I was obedient to His request and galloped on the endless beach until I got tired; then I walked back. Every time I ran, I left hoofprints in the sand and was able to gauge how far

I went. These hoofprints did not disappear, so that each time I ran, I saw that I went farther than the previous time. Then the Lord took me back to the stable. This happened day after day. Each time I outran the time before. All Jesus would ever say to me was *Run*.

Then one day, after He had said, *Run*, I decided to go off-course and run on top of the water. He never told me to run in the water; it was my choice. When I came back, Jesus was smiling. It was almost as if that is what He was waiting for all along. Then He hopped on and rode on my back while I ran on the water. Our movements merged and we were together as one.

I remember this word and think of it in times when I feel led to step out in faith for the impossible or when I want to try something that, to my knowledge, has never been done before. Life can seem like running as fast as possible in one direction as the Lord leads over and over again. In this prophetic picture, Jesus gave the command to run, just as a master gives a command to a servant. I was obedient to my master. It was not until I decided to explore and go off-course to investigate the impossible and follow my heart that Jesus went from being a proud master to being a friend who partnered in my desire for adventure. I believe that is what He wants for us today. He wants us to explore impossibilities and wild adventures with Him. He wants us to be so far out there in believing that He can do anything that if we run on top of the water, He is there, not from the sidelines cheering us on but riding with us as one.

We can live safe, comfortable and obedient lives with limited risk taking, knowing God is good, and that could be fine. But I would rather follow my heart and attempt to run on top of the water, trusting Him to empower and anoint me to do the impossible, than sit at home with no scars or stories to tell. God loves to move on our behalf when we step out into new realms of impossibilities, trusting in Him completely.

I believe we are entering into an age when Jesus is waiting for us to leave the places where we feel safe so that we can journey with Him on the dangerous waters. We are embarking on a season when it is our time to run on the water and to do the impossible, all for His glory. This joy-filled adventure on top of the water is in addition to and goes beyond healing the sick, casting out demons and other spiritual endeavors. We are now entering an era of seeing God do miracles on our behalf simply because He is in love with us and wants us to enjoy Him. Jesus is waiting for us to follow our hearts to be with Him in the most unlikely of places. He wants to partner with us. It is now time to discover the wildness of His heart in the secret places.

ACTIVATION: **Follow Your Heart**

It is crucial to pay attention to the desires and dreams deep within our hearts. It is also important to follow our hearts in moving closer to Jesus, just as Peter did, no matter what it might look like. Peter was led by his heart, not his head. He did not try to figure everything out first before stepping out of the boat. There is something special about his passionate impulsivity and desperation simply to be closer to his friend Jesus. If he had not followed his heart, his moment of doing the impossible would never have happened.

There is a reason why you like certain things, are drawn to certain people and have specific desires deep within you. You owe it to yourself and to the world to explore why that is. Not everyone has a desire to walk on water like Peter did, write a book about revivals like I did or have a son like

Hannah did. Some people have a desire to go into the African bush to reach people with the love of Jesus. Others want to be nurses or lawyers or mothers or Olympians. There is something unique inside of you that God placed there when He knit you together in your mother's womb. It is crucial to explore and discover why those desires are there and how you can steward those dreams to fulfillment.

Following your refined heart will position you to step into the impossible. Jesus is waiting for you, just as He was waiting for Peter, to begin to walk on water and to meet Him in the secret places of His heart.

1. If you had unlimited resources, time, energy, money, courage, what would you do with your life?

2. Write out 25 dreams or goals in your heart that have yet to be fulfilled. Make these personal to you. You might have a dream to go to Hawaii, get married, see your family come to know Jesus, ride a horse for the first time, paraglide, etc. These can be as diverse as you want. Do not feel the need to limit these to 25—add as many as you like and do not forget to dream big.

   When you have written these out, spend some time praying over them. Watch and see what God does as you dream with Him. As time goes on, it is super fun to look back and begin checking off fulfilled dreams and praising God. Some of these dreams you will be able to check off in less than a year; others might take more than ten years, like one of mine. Do not worry about the timeline for fulfillment; simply entrust these seeds to the Lord and His process.

10

Risk

Life is boring if we never take risks to follow our hearts. John Wimber (1934–1997), leader of the Vineyard movement, liked to say that faith is spelled *R-I-S-K*. Faith is believing in what is unseen and acting upon it (see Hebrews 11). It appears to me that many times miracles and risk taking go hand in hand. It all starts with taking that first step into the infinite abyss of uncertainty and completely relying on Jesus. The vulnerable act of stepping out in faith makes life extremely dangerous, exciting and breathtaking. Sometimes we will have to be willing to sacrifice something great to step out into the unknown, where we think the Lord might be leading us. There is great risk in this, because the outcome can be potential devastation or great triumph. I have noticed, though, that the greater the risk, the greater the reward will be.

Peter could not have walked on water if he had never taken the first step. Many people are waiting for everything to make sense before they risk and step out of the boat to follow Jesus; the funny thing is, with Jesus many times it never will make sense. Proverbs 3:5–6 says, "Trust in the LORD with all your heart and lean not on your own understanding; in all your ways acknowledge him, and he will make your paths straight." There is something powerful about following Jesus wholeheartedly even when the circumstances do not line up.

It is okay if we have no idea what is going on or if we do not know why we are doing what He is asking us to do in the moment. We do not need to know the end result, the answer or how it will all work before we step out of the boat to follow our hearts to be with Jesus. When Jesus gives the word to come closer to Him, even if we cannot logically find any good reason for doing so, we can trust that, as we take the first step toward Him, He will keep us above the waters. Jesus is waiting for us to let go and to risk so that He can do the impossible on our behalf.

Twentieth Anniversary in Toronto

One time I stepped out of the boat was in January 2014 to be a part of the twentieth anniversary of the Toronto Blessing in Toronto, Ontario, Canada. I had never been there, but many of my friends had testified how this move of God had brought renewal and a fresh awakening in their spirits. Around this time, I had been studying and writing about revivalists like Rees Howells and others who stepped out in faith to follow their hearts. Through my learning about their stories, the Lord was strengthening my faith and preparing me to do the same.

I did not have the resources to go to Toronto, but I believed that if God had called me to go and put it in my heart, He would make a way. I decided to use my airline points and pay the few hundred dollars more that I needed to book the ticket. When I tried to book my ticket online, my bank account did not have sufficient funds to cover it, because my paycheck had not yet been deposited. I started to look into the mistake and discovered that my ticket was already purchased and only $66 had been charged to my account. I called the airline, the points people and any other number I could find to make sure I had really paid for the ticket and would not get charged a huge amount later on. They all said the same thing: The ticket was already purchased for $66, and I was all set. Bonus!

The registration fee for the twentieth-anniversary celebration conference was more than $200, if I remember right. I did not have those funds yet, but I decided to fly to Canada anyway, trusting that God would make a way once I was there. On top of that, nearly all of the hotel rooms in the area were booked. Because I was going by myself, it was very expensive per night for the hotel. Nevertheless, I booked the first three nights by faith. I was not sure what I was going to do for the other three nights I needed to stay, but I decided to trust the Lord.

I went to the service at Catch the Fire, the church that hosted the Toronto Blessing, on Sunday morning after I arrived. There I connected with some of the media team about a research project I was working on that related to the beginnings of the Toronto Blessing. I noticed there was favor in our conversation, so I stepped out of the boat again. I asked if they would be willing to let me make a trade and do some research for them. I was overwhelmed and blessed by their generosity—they gave me access to the conference and the media library so I could attend the conference for free, as well as do some much-needed research on my own project with their primary sources. This was great news!

Then, when it was nearing the time when I would no longer be able to afford the hotel room, a friend decided at the last minute to fly out and meet me there to attend the conference. We split the cost of the room, which allowed me to stay longer. She left to go home during the last two days of my stay, and I did not have enough for a hotel room by myself. I was faced with a decision: Would I trust God to provide, or would I put the hotel room on my credit card? There have been times in my life when I actually felt the grace and peace to put something on my credit card and pay it off later. This time, however, I felt the Lord asking me to step outside of the boat one more time to rely on Him alone.

I let go of staying in the hotel room, without any idea where I was going to sleep that night. I ran into one of my friends who was a part of the Iris Global family, who invited me to stay in her hotel for the night because she had extra space. The night after that, I ran into someone else with Iris Global, who had booked an extra room that could not be refunded, so that person blessed a friend and me with a hotel suite. Each time I waited on the Lord, He upgraded the room. The last two nights I stayed in Toronto, I stayed for free. I could have played it safe in the boat and paid for my own hotel room with my credit card, but instead I stepped out of the boat, and the Lord provided yet again, primarily through the Body of Christ.

I had many moments of stepping out of the boat on this trip. It seemed like each step, each risk, was necessary to position me for the next breakthrough. First the $66 airline ticket, then the conference ticket and then the hotel rooms. The whole Toronto trip—let alone the conference, which was amazing—marked me with the reality that God is the God of the impossible, who loves to back us up when we step outside of the boat to follow Him into uncertain waters.

Ignite Azusa

I had another opportunity to step out of the boat to follow the leading of the Lord in late 2015. Lou Engle with The-Call, along with Iris Global, Bethel School of Supernatural Ministry, Youth With A Mission and many other streams, were preparing to partner together on the 110th anniversary of the Azusa Street revival for an event in Los Angeles called Azusa Now. I was excited to be a part of what God wanted to pour out, and I could feel the synergy and momentum in the Spirit leading toward that day.

Much of my Ph.D. work was in the origins of Pentecostalism, and many Pentecostal ministries find their roots in or were significantly influenced by the Azusa Street revival, which started in 1906. Many of my colleagues are the historians and theologians who helped write this revival into the history books. Knowing as much as I did about the origins of the Azusa Street revival and then seeing so many of the people I knew and loved getting excited about what God wanted to do at the 110th anniversary thrilled me.

I wanted to partner with this move of God as best I could with the gifts God had given me. I love writing about revival history, and in late 2015 after a conversation with Lou Engle, the idea came to write a short history of the Azusa Street revival. It was my hope that as many people as possible before the event would read more about this well of revival so we could go deeper and build upon what God had initiated 110 years before.

The only problem was that the event was to be held on April 9, 2016. This meant that I would need to have the book written by February—only a couple of months away—to get it printed, published and distributed before the big day. I was already doing some editing work and helping a spiritual father with some of his books when the idea to write about Azusa came into my heart. With the event looming, I knew that I would not be able to continue working for him and write a book about Azusa at the same time. This project would take 100 percent of my focus. To do the impossible, I knew I would have to lay everything else aside.

The first book I had written took me more than seven years to write. I have written other books since then that took anywhere from six months to three years. I was not sure it would be possible to write the book in that short amount of time or if there would even be outlets for distributing it. I did not want to let my spiritual father down by stopping my work for him, especially if I ended up not being able to finish the book on Azusa anyway. Further, I would be stepping out of the boat financially as well; writing the Azusa history would cost me because I would not be getting paid for a few months while I fully invested in this project. Additionally, I would have to pay for cover design, formatting, rights for the pictures, printing and other costs related to the book.

It was a big risk. I struggled with the thought of letting down this spiritual father, who had been there for me in tough times. Feeling torn apart inside, I finally mustered enough courage to share my heart with him. I told him that I needed to take a break to try to immerse myself completely in this Azusa project to see if God might make a way. He was gracious and supportive and championed me in my endeavors. By the time I finally committed to the project and jumped in, I really only had about two months to write the book before it would need to be formatted and printed in time for the event. I rearranged my schedule and cut out a lot of excess in my life for that season, believing that God would empower me to do the impossible by His strength.

I focused intently on this project each day and had an incredible team of people interceding for me as well as helping me in other ways. I am tremendously grateful for the team God brought and how hard they worked to see His heart released through this book. Some funding came in from supporters to help cover a good portion of the book's expenses, which made it possible to get more copies distributed. The printers even saw God's hand on this project and donated a few hundred copies to bless us.

A few weeks after the files were submitted and literally days before all the ministry school students left on their ministry trips to Azusa, we received the printed books and were able to distribute them to everyone in the school. For all this to come together as quickly as it did in such a short amount of time was truly impossible. I needed at least six more months to write *Ignite Azusa: Positioning for a New Jesus Revolution*; there is no way that book should have been complete in two months. Without God, it was truly impossible. Every time I think about it, I am humbled, overwhelmed and in awe of God's great love, faithfulness and power to complete this assignment. As of this writing, *Ignite Azusa* has already been translated into German and Portuguese. The testimony of writing *Ignite Azusa* may not seem especially miraculous to you, but as a writer I know that what I experienced was a true miracle.

Peter was a fisherman, and when Jesus told him to throw his net on the other side of the boat and he pulled in a multitude of fish, he knew that he had just experienced a miracle. Another time Jesus told Peter and the other disciples to feed a multitude of more than five thousand people with only five loaves of bread and two fish. Jesus later told Peter to catch a fish with a gold coin in its mouth to pay his taxes (Matthew 17:24–27). Each of these stories of Jesus activating

Peter's faith ties in to his previous profession as a fisherman. Miracles come in all different shapes and sizes. If we have eyes to see and courage to take the first step, we might begin to see even more in our everyday lives and workplaces.

ACTIVATION: Taking Your First Step

1. From your previous list of dreams, which one is the Lord highlighting the most right now?

2. What can you do today to take the first step toward this dream?

3. What will your life look like in ten years if you never take that first step?

4. Whom can you share your dream with to help keep you accountable to steward the promises of God in your life?

I encourage you to take the first step this week toward the impossible dream God has put in your heart. God can always redirect a moving ship, but one that is safe in the harbor is not going anywhere. I pray and declare that this one step creates an unstoppable momentum in your life and an acceleration toward a greater destiny than you could ever hope, dream or imagine.

11

Resilience

As we embrace a lifestyle of faith and step out to take more risks, it is highly probable that we will fall in the process. Risking, being vulnerable and stepping out in faith guarantee some measure of failure. But following our hearts closer to Jesus even when it makes no sense at all attracts the heart of God to do the impossible.

On this journey toward walking in the impossible on a more regular basis, it is important to remember that when you fall (and you will), make sure you always fall forward and get back up. I am not talking about falling into sin or immorality, but about falling when you have taken a step of faith in one direction and it does not turn out the way you had hoped. If you can learn to navigate through disappointment, get back up, learn from the experience and move forward, you will grow in faith and be better prepared to step into the impossible in the future.

When we fall and disappointment comes, there is a danger of retreating and taking fewer risks because of a few failed attempts. The only way to grow in faith, however, is to risk. This means you will get dirty from falling and will likely get bruises from time to time. You can stay unscathed by sitting still all your life, or you can risk, deal with disappointment, learn from it, grieve the loss and continue venturing into the unknown, exploring different expressions of God's heart in this world.

In 1910, Theodore Roosevelt gave a speech in Paris, France, about the beauty and pain of risk taking. He said,

> It is not the critic who counts; not the man who points out how the strong man stumbles, or where the doer of deeds could have done them better. The credit belongs to the man who is actually in the arena, whose face is marred by dust and sweat and blood; who strives valiantly; who errs, who comes short again and again, because there is no effort without error and shortcoming; but who does actually strive to do the deeds; who knows great enthusiasms, the great devotions; who spends himself in a worthy cause; who at the best knows in the end the triumph of high achievement, and who at the worst, if he fails, at least fails while daring greatly, so that his place shall never be with those cold and timid souls who neither know victory nor defeat.[1]

It is far better to have loved and lost, to have tried and failed, to have followed your heart to a closed door than to live with painful regrets of never knowing what could have been. I believe God is waiting for us to more regularly follow our hearts and to step out in faith so that He can do the impossible on our behalf.

Point of No Return

Life is always much more exciting when we position ourselves in such a way that Jesus has to show up or else we might drown. How often do we step so far out in faith that it requires God to move on our behalf or else we fail? How many programs at our churches need God to show up powerfully or they will fail? How many times do we step out toward the impossible where Jesus is our only option? When is the last time you got out of the boat to risk and be vulnerable with following your heart in such a way that if God did not back you up, you would look like a fool, risk your reputation, lose your job or be rejected?

Peter ventured to the place of no return, where Jesus became his only option. He put himself between the boat and Jesus. He literally needed Jesus to sustain his every step. This is complete reliance on the Savior. Each one of Peter's steps was totally dependent on the authority of Jesus. Peter could not move forward without complete trust in Jesus. As he fixed his eyes on Jesus, he continued to do the impossible, step by step.

I do not ever want to get in a place in ministry where I can rely upon my own talents to touch the hearts of people. God *has* to show up. He is the point of it all. If His manifest presence does not come into a meeting I am leading, there is no reason to gather. I need to be fully possessed by the Spirit and anointed by Jesus to have anything of significance to say. He is my every breath. There is no reason to go to church if there is no expectation of actually encountering God there. I do not want to live a life where I can just learn more about Jesus; I want more of Him. I do not want a life of safety and comfort, devoid of risk. I want to go on adventures with Jesus where He has to meet me on the waters or else I might sink and drown because I am too far out searching for Him in the deep places. I want to live a lifestyle of risk taking in which I am so in love with Jesus that walking on water becomes second nature to me.

Fall Forward

"But when he saw the wind, he was afraid and, beginning to sink, cried out, 'Lord, save me!' Immediately Jesus reached out his hand and caught him. 'You of little faith,' he said, 'why did you doubt?'" (Matthew 14:30–31).

Peter took a risk by getting out of the boat. He was compelled to be closer to Jesus. He was far enough away from the boat that when he took his eyes off Jesus and started to sink, his only option was to fall forward toward Him. He was too far out to retreat to the boat. He had ventured into the realm of impossibility, to the point of no return, where Jesus became his only source of deliverance.

When Peter did lose his focus on Jesus, he fell forward into His arms rather than backward. Peter was totally abandoned to Jesus to the place where if Jesus did not rescue him, he could have drowned. If we take great risks and find ourselves in over our heads or have a moment of doubt, as long as we fall forward and lean into Jesus, He will immediately be there for us. There was no delay. Jesus was right there to rescue His friend Peter.

Little Faith?

Even though Peter did what no other person had done besides Jesus Himself, he was rebuked for his "little faith." To be honest, I would have thought Peter would have been celebrated for his ridiculous faith. No other disciple had that reckless courage and devotion to Jesus just then. Peter literally did the impossible for a moment. What great courage! I would have wanted to shake his hand or pat him on the back for at least attempting such a feat.

And yet, after Jesus immediately came to his rescue, He rebuked him. I do not know about you, but if I had just been so vulnerable as to put my life in greater danger to be closer to Jesus, I would have felt confused, humiliated and possibly offended by His response in the midst of the stormy sea. But if I put myself in Jesus' shoes (or maybe sandals is a better way to put it), compassion may have welled up inside of me. Jesus longed for His friend—one of the three intimate ones He had invited even deeper into His heart—to see and understand what was readily available to him if he had just believed. Jesus knew how awesome it was to walk on water and to have authority over the storms. To share that experience with a friend must have been such joy. It appears that Jesus would have loved for Peter to walk on water even longer. By losing focus in the moment, however, Peter missed out on the fullness of what could have been his.

Jesus Expects Us to Do the Impossible

Jesus' unexpected rebuke in the midst of superseding the laws of nature is profound for several reasons. This rebuke speaks to the fact that Jesus expected Peter to do the impossible. Peter could have continued to walk on the sea if he had kept his focus on Jesus and not doubted. Jesus was not surprised when Peter walked on water but was saddened when he did not continue. Jesus knew that all things were possible for the ones who believed. He knew the power contained inside of Him.

Even after Peter had displayed what many of us today would call great faith, Jesus said, "You of little faith." If Peter had "little faith" and could walk on water, I cannot imagine what great faith could do! But again we see Jesus' heart revealed when He said, "You of little faith, why did you doubt?" I imagine Jesus' inner dialogue to have been something like this: *Why did you doubt, Peter? You started off strong, you had courage to step outside the boat, you kept your eyes on Me and not on the storms, you continued in forward momentum toward Me and you were doing the impossible. Why didn't you continue fixing your eyes on Me and trusting Me? Why did you doubt that I could sustain you in the midst of the sea?*

Jesus' rebuke makes me think of how many times in my own life I have started out strong with great faith to take risks, be vulnerable and move in the direction I felt the Holy Spirit was leading, but when I came up against resistance, distractions or fears, I lost hope and gave up. I allowed these moments of discouragement to steal my confidence.

How many of us have started off strong, stepped outside the boat and moved toward Jesus but then retreated when we saw the storm or got injured along the way? How many of us have felt led to take a risk when everyone around us thought we were crazy, and when we came up against resistance, we second-guessed ourselves and doubted whether He said, *Come*, in the first place? How many dreams have we sabotaged because we have allowed the storms of life to intimidate us or cloud our vision? Jesus expects us to initiate with Him to do the impossible. He does not just want us to have an impulsive surge of faith at the beginning of great acts of faith; He wants us to have sustained belief that remains focused on Him the whole time.

Shame Did Not Hold Peter Back

One of the beautiful features of this account is that once Jesus rescued Peter, they both still needed to walk back to the boat; but this time they did it together. Another special part of this story is that even though Peter stepped out in courageous vulnerability, started to sink and then got rebuked in front of his friends, he did not take offense at Jesus. He realized he had an opportunity to grow in greater faith. He continued to move forward.

Later, in Matthew 17, Peter got rebuked at the Transfiguration for not keeping his mouth shut. He also got rebuked after trying to defend Jesus by cutting off a soldier's ear (John 18:10–11). Then there was the devastating incident when Peter disowned Jesus three times in the moment he was needed most. I cannot imagine that look Peter got from Jesus after the third denial:

> Peter replied, "Man, I don't know what you're talking about!" Just as he was speaking, the rooster crowed. The Lord turned and looked straight at Peter. Then Peter remembered the word the Lord had spoken to him: "Before the rooster crows today, you will disown me three times." And he went outside and wept bitterly.
>
> Luke 22:60–62

At this later point in Peter's life, he could have let shame hold him back from Jesus. But he never did. Whenever Peter started to "sink" and got rebuked, over and over again he just got back up and continued on with Jesus. He had already left all to follow Him and did not have anywhere else to go. He trusted that Love Himself was shaping him. He learned not to limit himself by focusing on his shortcomings but rather chose to keep his eyes on Jesus.

Shame and self-pity are actually forms of pride. These cause us to focus on ourselves rather than on God and His goodness. Do not let shame bind you any longer. Peter didn't. He made mistakes and fell time and time again. But his strength lay in the fact that he fell forward, got back up and continued toward Jesus, no matter how many times he messed up on the way.

After Jesus' resurrection, Peter grew in greater faith than ever before:

> When they came back from the tomb, they told all these things to the Eleven and to all the others. It was Mary Magdalene, Joanna, Mary the mother of James, and the others with them who told this to the apostles. But they did not believe the women, because their words seemed to them like nonsense. Peter, however, got up and ran to the tomb. Bending over, he saw the strips of linen lying by themselves, and he went away, wondering to himself what had happened.
>
> Luke 24:9–12

Peter ran! He did not let his past inhibit his future and his destiny. He received the grace, mercy, love and forgiveness of Jesus and allowed love to compel him forward even through his shame. When everyone else thought the women's stories were nonsense, Peter believed and he ran.

Even the angels specifically wanted Peter to receive the message about Jesus' resurrection when they told the women, "But go, tell his disciples and Peter" (Mark 16:7). I love how the Lord picks the most unlikely of heroes. Peter, an impulsive fisherman who made messes wherever he went, was given the keys to the Kingdom of heaven (Matthew 16:17–19).

In one moment Peter was filled with boldness, walked on water and triumphed over nature, and in another he was filled with fear, started to sink, was rescued and then was rebuked by Jesus. A hero in one moment, humbled the next. The abundant life that Jesus died for us to have in John 10:10 is filled with joy and pain, hope and loss, success and misunderstanding, risk and suffering. This is the full life that

Jesus modeled. Many times the impossible can be messy and filled with all sorts of extremes. This is normal. Always remember, however, that it was Peter, the one who was not afraid of falling, who got to do the impossible while the others watched on.

ACTIVATION: Time to Get Back Up

Greatness is on the other side of getting back up just one more time. I once heard Heidi Baker say, "If you don't quit, you win." No matter how many times you have fallen, I encourage you to get back up. Do not let shame, fear, disappointment or anything else keep you down or hold you back from stepping out in faith again.

1. Is there anything from the past holding you back from all that God has for you today? Is there any place where you have failed or fallen short that you need to forgive yourself for and move on?

   If the Holy Spirit has highlighted any area where you have sinned, messed up or fallen short and you are still beating yourself up for it, I encourage you today to enter into a shame-free life, full of the love and freedom of the Father. Deal with this issue right away. Receive the forgiveness of Jesus. He has already paid the price for you to be free. The enemy wants you to keep this area a secret for as long as possible because he knows that once you bring it out into the light, the power to hold you down is immediately broken. Confession before the Lord brings forgiveness, and confession before our brothers and sisters in Christ brings healing. I encourage you to contact a trusted friend today to set up a time to share your heart, confess, process through it and receive prayer and forgiveness. You are important, and what you carry to impart to those around you and to the world is significant. Do not let anything from the past, where the enemy has tried to steal, kill and destroy, hold you back from your destiny (Jeremiah 29:11).

2. For those who have risked their hearts and experienced rejection, heartbreak and failure again and again, I celebrate you today and say there is hope! Sometimes the process to seeing these dreams fulfilled takes time. I rejoice in the fact that you have stepped out to risk your heart. You are truly on your way to see these dreams fulfilled and are better able to value, appreciate and steward them in the process.

   By continuing to cling to Jesus as we live through disappointments and failures, we will discover that closed doors and rejection are just redirection to something better. We have to dust ourselves off, get back up and continue on to discover what still awaits us. As long as we continue to move closer to Jesus, we will always be okay.

   Some of you reading this right now have had a time in your past when you had an incredible amount of courage and stepped out of the boat to risk and be with Jesus. In the process of being vulnerable and attempting to follow your heart, things did not end up working out, and you began to sink. Since that disappointment, which has cost you greatly, you have given up on stepping out of the boat again. Now is the time God wants to heal and restore your vulnerable heart. Jesus celebrates that risk and is calling you outside of the boat again. Ask Him to confirm the right timing to step out to Him into the extreme places. Keep your eyes on Jesus always, and if you stumble or fall on your way, call out to Him to catch you. He will be right there, waiting for you with open arms.

3. Declarations are powerful. They can help build you up in God's truth, and they are ready ammunition for when the enemy tries to knock you down with lies and accusations. Here are a few examples to get you started. Feel free to add personal ones that the Holy Spirit reveals to you (Ephesians 1 and Romans 8 are great places to start). Repeat these out loud daily to strengthen your spirit.

I declare that

I am free from shame.

I am forgiven because of the blood of Jesus.

I am accepted and loved.

I am an overcomer.

I am important, significant and treasured by God.

I am a target for God's blessings and favor.

I am worth the price that Jesus paid.

I am free to be me and to be fully loved.

I will never give up on the promises of God for my life.

I will get back up when I fall.

I will keep my eyes on Jesus always.

I will fulfill my God-given destiny no matter the price.

Nothing can separate me from the love of God.

Fear of failure is abolished from my life.

Love is my inheritance.

All of His promises over my life are yes and amen.

He will turn around every failure for good in His timing.

He will complete the work He started in me.

He will never leave nor forsake me.

He is always faithful.

12

Seek First the Kingdom

In Matthew 6:33, Jesus says, "But seek first his kingdom and his righteousness, and all these things will be given to you as well." As we take risks to step out in great faith, it is essential to be led by the Spirit and seek first His Kingdom. Our motivation should always be to grow closer to Jesus and to see His purposes fulfilled on the earth. Peter wanted to be closer to Jesus, and as a result of taking a risk toward that aim, he got to step into the impossible. His motivation was Jesus, not the impossible. Miracles are simply the fruit of intimacy with Jesus, not the goal of intimacy. We must keep this right perspective in line as we seek to be conduits for His Kingdom to come to earth.

Walking on Water in Indonesia

Evangelist Mel Tari shares a miracle his team experienced as a result of seeking first God's Kingdom. The team was journeying to an unreached people group in the area of

Timor in Indonesia so that they could preach the Gospel there. After walking all day, they ended up at the Noemina River, which they still needed to cross. This was during flood season, and the river was even higher than normal because it had rained quite a bit; at the time they arrived, the river was more than twenty feet deep and three hundred yards wide. The team was tired, so they planned to rest there a few days until the river went down. But suddenly they felt the Lord tell them to go immediately to the other side to minister to the people.

Mel's cousin was the first to step out in faith, even though many of the others on the team cautioned against it, fearing he might die. He put his foot in the river and then continued to walk across to the other side. The water level never came any higher than his knees, even though they had been told the river was anywhere from 20 to 25 feet deep during that season. The team followed, crossing the river in the same way, while the people who lived in that region watched. After they had crossed, the local people on the other side thought that maybe the river was not as deep as expected in that location, so they checked it out by walking into the water. They almost drowned, however, because the water was too deep. That was when they all realized that God had done a miracle to get them to the other side.[1]

In a village on the other side of the river, they preached the Gospel, and one person was even raised from the dead. Because of that miracle, the whole village got saved. In an interview, Mel shared that when the miracle was actually happening, his team did not realize it because their focus was not on the miracle; it was on the assignment God had given them to reach the people on the other side with the love of Jesus. Mel stressed the importance of seeking first the Kingdom:

131

The miracle is to facilitate us going from point A to point B to preach the Gospel. The miracle is not the end of itself, it is the means, it is the tool, it is the help that God has given us so that we can reach point B to preach the Gospel so that these people can come to the Lord. . . . The focus is always on Jesus and the mission. Miracles are the help and the tools that God sends our way so that we can accomplish the tasks, and the tasks are always so that the eternal destiny of mankind, they can come to know Jesus.[2]

Mel's team did not try to cross a river to see a miracle; they had to get to the other side so they could bring the Gospel of Jesus to an unreached people group. Much of the time, the impossible happens on the way to advancing God's Kingdom. Many times people are even unaware of the miracle until later, because it was never their focus.

Multiplication of Bread

When I lived in Mozambique in 2000, I spent some of my time helping bring food to people in refugee camps who had been displaced by devastating floods. After ministering with Heidi Baker and the team and seeing many people accept Jesus at one of the refugee camps, I felt a conviction to continue discipling these newborn Christians. I did not just want to bring them bread and lead them to Jesus only to leave them there alone, but God had also put it on my heart to help grow these people up in the Lord. Nearly every week for more than five months, I went back to that refugee camp, Camp 2000, and brought food, teams, doctors and pastors. I poured my life out for these people and helped plant a church there. I was 22 years old at the time.

One time, I brought a visiting team of students from Bethel School of Supernatural Ministry to Camp 2000 to help me minister. We bought bread for the hungry people. When we were about to pass out the loaves, we realized there were far more people than loaves of bread. One of the team asked me if we should break the bread in half before handing it out so that we could feed all the people. I recalled the stories of Jesus feeding the multitudes with only a few loaves. I told her that instead of tearing the pieces of bread in half, we would pray over them and ask God to feed all of the people there.

After we did this, we continued to minister and pass out bread. One by one, each person received a whole loaf until finally we had fed all of the people, and we even had many loaves left over.

The funny thing is, I did not even realize a miracle of bread multiplication had happened until we were back at the base a few days later and the team talked about it. Then it dawned on me that Jesus had multiplied the bread! We never planned to see that miracle; we just wanted everyone to eat. We were not going after a powerful testimony we could take back home with us; we simply saw hungry people in front of us who needed to be fed. We needed God to come through or else they could have starved; there were no other options. Our motivation was compassion. It was seeing Jesus in them and responding by stepping out in faith to do whatever possible to love them well. We sought first the Kingdom of God, and He responded.

Destiny House

Many years later, during an intense season of desperation, I stepped out in faith to follow the leading of the Holy Spirit despite unfavorable circumstances. I did not realize it at the time, but this was precisely when God catapulted me into

133

a greater measure of my destiny. In the fall of 2011, I had just returned to the United States after spending four years in England doing my Ph.D. work on the life and ministry of Carrie Judd Montgomery. After being introduced to the Bethel community in Mozambique years earlier, I felt it was time to explore what God might have for me in Redding, California. A friend I had met in Africa welcomed me to stay at her house for a time, which was an incredible gift.

I began to apply for various jobs to see if anything would open up, but one door after another closed. I was not sure what to do next, so I decided to find my people. I showed up at the local office of Heidi and Rolland Baker's ministry, Iris Global, and made myself available to serve. The staff was very gracious and welcomed me in. I spent much of the time writing thank-you postcards to their supporters. It was humbling, having just received a Ph.D. and following my heart to Redding, to find myself with no car and no job, sitting there day after day, writing thank-you postcards. But I had believed there was something worth exploring in Redding that would tie in to my destiny.

In October, I headed back to my hometown in Southern California for a wedding and also to connect with Heidi Baker after one of her meetings. I chose to be vulnerable, and through tears I shared my heart with her about my desire for more of a covering to fulfill the call of God I felt was on my life. She gladly and readily agreed to ordain me. I was greatly moved by her belief in me; I felt that I needed her blessing and impartation because of what I was about to step into, even though, at that point, I had no idea what that would be. My ordination took place on New Year's Eve in 2011 at Heidi's home in Redding. The night was unforgettable, a time of being marked powerfully by God as I entered into this new community.

Thankfully, as I sought to begin building a life in Redding, a friend I had met there, Carrie Grosch, agreed to let me stay with her for a month while I tried to figure out what that might look like. I stayed in her spare room and slept on an air mattress for the month of January 2012 while I job hunted and tried to find a car, since I had sold mine before I moved to England.

Toward the end of the month I had not yet found work or a car, and I was still living on an air mattress. One Sunday I could not even find a ride to church, so I walked the five and a half miles to get there and ended up making it for the night service. Being new in town with limited mobility and resources to my name was extremely trying. It was also incredibly stressful trying to find a car and a home at the same time that did not exceed the limited funds I had from selling off my 401(k). During this time, the Lord apprehended me by reminding me of Matthew 6:33. When I pondered what seeking first the Kingdom looked like in my situation, I felt that He was directing me to find a place to live before buying a car. This meant I needed to lay down my desire for the freedom of mobility and move wholeheartedly toward finding a home.

Then, through a couple of friends, God led me to a house for rent downtown on Placer Street (Placer also means "gold mine"). The home was way out of the price range I was hoping for, but it had everything on my list of desires, and I felt God on it. The three-story house was under renovation, and the apartment on the middle floor that I wanted would be ready in mid-February. I shared my heart with the owner, Brad Coulter, and asked if he would believe in my dream to launch people into their destinies from a community cultivated around God's presence. I also asked him to decrease the rent and include furniture, since I had none. Further, I had no car and no job, and he probably thought I was crazy. He said he would pray about it.

In the meantime, the end of January was approaching while things were still up in the air with the house on Placer Street. Carrie had been very gracious to let me stay with her, but now it was time to move on, and I was not sure what I was going to do. I wanted to honor her generosity in agreeing to let me stay for one month, so I found a room to rent in another house. Because I had no other options and did not know what else to do, in the moment, I said yes to the landlord. While this other room was perfect provision, as I moved in that direction, I did not have peace at all about living there. Even though it had a good price and would have been fine, I had not left everything behind to settle for something I knew was only silver, not gold.[3] I ran into Carrie on February 1, the day I was to move into the other house, and she saw that I was distraught over my decision. She gave me even more grace and extended my stay at her place a few extra days so that I could make a wiser decision.

Those days were rough. Have you ever been in a situation when you know you have overstayed your welcome but you do not know what else to do because breakthrough has not yet come? It was extremely humbling. I was learning for the first time what it meant to ask for help and to rely on the Body of Christ. Not many days after this, Heidi blessed me with a place to stay for a couple of weeks while I was believing to later transition to the house on Placer Street, which Brad had still not decided to rent to me. Once I had breakthrough to stay somewhere temporarily, a huge weight was lifted off and I felt like I could dream again. The same evening that happened, God gave me the idea to host missionaries in the Placer home to celebrate and honor them for their lives of sacrifice. I called Brad the next day and shared the vision, telling him I was now certain I wanted to rent the middle floor. By that point, he already had a family ready to take it who had their own furniture and were willing to pay the full rent.

This grieved my soul. The Holy Spirit was compelling me toward this house. I saw destiny all over this place but had no idea how it would become a reality. I knew I needed to contend for this house because God had a purpose, mission and divine destiny for it. Then Brad had a divine appointment. He took a wrong turn to his bank, but on the way he intercepted a missionary from Africa, with whom he shared the vision God had given me. She wept and said she wished there had been a place like that for her many years ago. That won him over. The Lord had redirected him so he would say yes to renting the apartment to me.

At that time, all the money I had would go toward the deposit and the first month's rent; I had no idea how I was going to get enough money to pay for the second month's rent. The other ladies who were thinking of living there with me backed out, one just a day before we were to move in. Even in that, the Lord put determination inside of me to contend. Not long after, I got a call from a complete stranger who was willing to partner with the vision. Eventually God brought others who would be called to carry the vision and steward the well of revival there.

As I stepped out in faith toward this dream, I remembered the testimony of Carrie Judd Montgomery, who likewise stepped out in faith in the 1880s to plant one of the first healing homes on the East Coast in her early twenties. She had enough money for only the first few months' rent, but from her act of faith, her healing homes have continued to this day. The Home of Peace, established in 1893, is still operating in Oakland, California. I thought to myself, *If she can do it, then I can, as well.* Her story strengthened my resolve to step out of the boat even though I only had enough money to cover one month's rent in the home. Praise the Lord! He has since come through every month, sometimes miraculously.

This home and community has now become known as Destiny House. We started with three people on the middle floor. After the first six months, we acquired the downstairs and grew to nine. Two years later, we were able to rent the upstairs when a family moved in. This meant that all three floors were unified in worshiping Jesus and hosting God's presence together. Since then we have inspired several other homes to be birthed that carry similar DNA, and we have even planted a Destiny House internationally.

We currently have a one-hundred-year vision for worship to be released within the context of family in our home and for five thousand worshiping communities to be launched around the world. We worship and minister as a community every Friday morning in our living room, and each time is unique and special. These meetings are open for visitors to join us. Our only agenda on Fridays is to worship Jesus and encounter God together.

In February 2017, we celebrated the fifth anniversary of Destiny House. None of this would have been possible without the countless saints that God has brought to steward this vision along the way, who sought first the Kingdom and courageously stepped out in faith to partner with what God was doing. We have seen missionaries blessed and sent out, people healed, debts paid off, creativity released and songs birthed. We have had overshadowing times of worship, when the glory of God was so thick we were on our faces and could only whisper for the rest of the day. We have seen people feel so safe and covered in God's love that they have stepped out in faith to do things they never thought possible. Many have had profound encounters with God's love in this home.

One morning, a burned-out missionary suffering from post-traumatic stress disorder, Jessika Tate, showed up because an acquaintance of hers had had a dream that Jessika was supposed to visit Destiny House. Jessika was healed when one of our ladies, Katharina Welt, danced over her during worship.[4] This is just one of the many healings people have experienced there. People have come from around the world to drink and partake of God's presence in this well.

The Lord has been so good. He has done miracle after miracle at Destiny House, and it all started with one little yes to seek first His Kingdom. Many other yeses soon followed. This ministry would not have impacted as many people or be what it is today without the Body of Christ coming together, each person playing his or her part.

The thing I want to highlight in this story is that when I stepped out in faith to get the house, I did not set out to establish a movement of worshiping communities around the world. I simply wanted a home where I could thrive and have people over to worship regularly. I wanted a place where I could fully be me and fulfill my calling. I had been discipling women for nearly twenty years, and the dream of living with them in community always appealed to me. My motivation was simply to live the abundant life Jesus died for me to have and not to settle for anything less. I was simply following my heart and the direction I felt the Spirit leading me at that time.

People ask me how I strategized to see this vision of Destiny House fulfilled. I laugh because I remember the complete and utter mess I was in, the place of total surrender, desperation and dependence on God and His Body. I was struggling just to keep my head above water and to survive when the breakthrough emerged. Through the Lord's mercy, He allowed me to tap in to a deep well that existed long before I had ever arrived to the scene. All I wanted was a home. I knew I had to stay true to my core value of not settling for silver when I am destined for gold, so I chose to say no to the other place before knowing what would be next. Pioneering Destiny House was not easy at all. It was like giving birth—it was painful and messy at times, and I was completely vulnerable. I gave up everything and relied completely on Jesus and the Body of Christ each month to come through. As I was faithful to seek first His Kingdom and follow the leading of the Holy Spirit, all these things and more were added unto me, just as His Word promises.

Further, the story of me going for the home before the car is entirely prophetic. We need family (a home) before we need ministry (a car). Ministry and fruitfulness flow from intimacy with God and also from the place of being knit together with the family of God. What is now known as Destiny House was launched from a place of family. As I and many others sought first the Kingdom, God backed us up to do the impossible again and again. When not just one person seeks first the Kingdom of God, but a community does this together, it expands our capacity to carry what God wants to release; He longs to increase the weight of glory upon our lives. Seeking Him first in and with family will take you places you could never go on your own, beyond your wildest dreams. That is what happened to us in the founding of the Destiny House movement. And this is only the beginning.

ACTIVATION: Led by the Spirit

Just as Peter followed his heart and ended up doing the impossible, as we seek first the Kingdom and follow our hearts, we will also step into miracles, signs and wonders without even realizing it. Jesus must always remain our focus and motivation for the impossible. When our eyes are fixed on Him and we are intent on giving Him all of the glory, He moves on our behalf. When the family of God partners together to take steps of faith to seek first His Kingdom, corporately we can step into an even greater measure of the fullness of our destinies and release even more of His heart to this generation.

1. What does it look like to be led of the Spirit and to seek first the Kingdom of heaven today, even if things do not make sense?

2. How can you seek first the Kingdom in your family, job, relationships, passions and desires this week?

3. Just one yes can change the world and impact generations. What is God calling you to say yes to today? And how can you say yes to those God has highlighted for you to run with in this season?

13

Miracle Flight

We need family to step into the fullness of our destiny. We can only go so far alone, but when we link arms with the family of God, we can soar beyond our wildest dreams. One of the hardest lessons I learned in the process of birthing Destiny House was the need to ask for help from the Body of Christ. I had previously thought that God and I could take on the world by ourselves. That experience awakened me to the reality that I also need people in my life to fulfill His purposes. In the process of risking to follow my heart, I had to learn to ask for help and, even more so, learn to receive love. Something beautiful emerges through interdependence, and I think God intended it that way.

In May 2014, I experienced even more how much God loves to use the family of Christ as agents for birthing the miraculous. When I again put myself out there in a similar way to Peter, stepping off the boat by faith, I learned even more that had it not been for the Body of Christ stepping in to lend a helping hand, I would not have experienced breakthrough.

I had a desire to return to England for a wedding and to reconnect with my friends there. I had not been back to England for nearly three years, since completing my Ph.D. As the wedding approached, it was literally impossible for me to afford the trip because I had recently finished a work project and was still in search of my next paid assignment from the Lord. I did not even have enough money to pay the following month's rent. I had no other options for help but God and the Body of Christ. Even so, for several months leading up to the wedding, I felt peace that I would be in England to take part in the celebration. I even RSVP'd to the wedding by faith months before. I was so determined to be there, I told God that even if it meant having my bags packed and showing up at the airport without a ticket, I would do everything possible on my side to position myself to receive this miracle.

And it looked like I might have to do just that. While I was praying for financial breakthrough, the exact opposite happened—I got hit with unexpected taxes and ended up owing a couple thousand dollars that I was not prepared for. I had a choice then: Would I let this setback sabotage my dream to go back to England, or would I keep believing for a way to get to the wedding? I was not going to let my circumstances hold me back from trusting that God could make a way where there was no way.

The week leading up to the wedding, I still had not received the financial breakthrough I had been praying for to be able to buy an airplane ticket. But I continued to plan and live my life as if I would be there anyway, because I really felt that God was sending me for such a time as this. On the Monday before the wedding, by faith I sent out my newsletter announcing that I would be in England later that week. I felt I needed to do this as a declaration over my life and as an act of faith, believing that what was in my heart was also in His and would come to pass in His way. I also posted the following declaration over my situation on social media: "When you have no other options but God and the Body of Christ, something beautiful is bound to happen. . . ." This truth had been ingrained in me in a powerful way since the Destiny House breakthrough.

Since the wedding was that Friday, May 30, I had arranged to start my journey to the airport on Tuesday to make a flight by Wednesday. When Tuesday morning came and I was getting ready to go, however, I hesitated. I thought I needed to do more research on airfares to be better prepared. As I began my research, though, I felt unrest and sensed this thinking was filled with doubt and fear. After going back and forth about when to leave, I looked at my bank account and realized I had no other options. My financial situation was impossible even if I stayed in California. I did not even have enough money in my account to get groceries.

I felt that the financial breakthrough I needed would be on the other side of this faith journey. With my bags packed and my last full tank of gas in my car, I decided to step out toward what I believed was part of my destiny for this time in my life. I knew that the longer I delayed, the more my faith would diminish, and I might miss God's timing. I was compelled by the Spirit to head to the airport. I invited some of our Destiny House family, Matt and Lisa Shutte and Brittany Oelze, to come along for this faith adventure.

On the Way

In the Bible, I have noticed that many miracles happened "on the way" when people responded in faith to move in the direction God commanded. In Luke 17:11–19, it was not until the lepers responded to Jesus' instructions to show

themselves to the priests that they were healed—on the way.
I was similarly praying for breakthrough to happen on the
way as I stepped out in faith and headed toward San Francisco International Airport. During the car ride, we saw a
beautiful and strange-looking sliver of a rainbow in the sky
without any rain in sight. I received this as a promise from
God. Then I got a call about an offer to teach in the fall. A
promise in the sky and job breakthrough were a great start
to this adventure into the impossible!

The drive from Redding to San Francisco is about three
and a half hours. When I travel there, many times I like to
stop on the way at the Home of Peace in Oakland, founded
by Carrie Judd Montgomery. I wanted to tap in to this his-
toric revival well because it has been a launching pad for
missionaries and leaders from around the world for generations. Almost immediately after we arrived, someone pulled
me aside and handed me a check for $500 toward my trip! If
I had hesitated or waited to go on my journey the next day, I
would have missed this person, since she and her family were
leaving early the next morning for a vacation. Praise God for
giving more confirmation and providing through the Body
of Christ! I did not feel the need to rush to the airport that
night, and I was blessed to have someone cover my room for
the night there, so we spent the evening resting and catching
up with some good friends.

The next morning, we spent time in the chapel soaking in
God's glory and enjoying being in His presence together as
family as we prepared to leave for the airport. I sent a text
message to a friend at 10:42 a.m. that said,

> Going to spend some time in the chapel at the Home of Peace
> worshiping with some of the Destiny House family and then
> will get dropped off at San Francisco Airport.

> I am believing God will make a way and that this testimony
> will be sent out to dismantle strongholds of fear and infuse
> this generation with hope in a God who loves to love us!

This message was a declaration of hope over my situation for what I believed God would do. For the whole month leading up to that day, I had been meditating on Isaiah 43, about how God did the impossible miracle of parting the Red Sea for Moses and the Israelites. That morning we were not calling out to God for breakthrough but simply feasting on Him and His goodness, thanking Him ahead of time for the miracle He was about to perform.

After our time of worship at Carrie Judd Montgomery's home of legacy, it was go time. I had to get on a flight by that afternoon or I would not make the wedding. At noon, we left the chapel, and when we walked out the doors and toward the car, my stomach dropped. It felt like the time I went skydiving and was about to jump out of the plane. I was once again about to take a huge leap of faith. If God did not show up to catch me or give me wings to soar, I would look like a fool. He was my only option. I was about to venture into territory I had never been to before.

At this point, there was just enough gas in the tank to get us to the airport, and I now had $500 toward a ticket that would cost more than $1,500. I enlisted many of my prayer warrior friends as we headed to the airport. Earlier in the week, I had asked Heidi Baker, who had done this several times in the past, to share a testimony and pray for me on my journey. She shared how one time she only had $100 but felt led to go from Los Angeles to New York. She showed up at Los Angeles International Airport, and while she was there, a sale on tickets from Los Angeles to New York showed up for $99. I recalled her testimony time and time again to strengthen myself in the Lord as I headed toward the impossibility that awaited me.

No Open Doors

When I arrived at San Francisco International Airport, I thanked Matt, Lisa and Brittany and encouraged them to tour the Golden Gate Bridge. But I asked them not to leave town until they heard from me in case I did not make it on the plane. They insisted on joining me all the way through this adventure and accompanied me inside the airport. This made things even more awkward because I had no idea what I was doing, and now I had an audience. While it was uncomfortable at first, I am grateful they stayed, because I needed their prayers and support throughout the journey.

When I walked into the airport, I felt led to get in line at United Airlines first. I walked up to the counter and handed the man my passport. He asked where I was headed. I told him I was going to London. I wondered if by some miracle a ticket would appear as he typed in my passport information. He could not find one, though. Then I told him I was interested in learning how to fly standby. He looked on his computer and noticed that plenty of standby tickets were available, which was great news. Then he asked me who my buddy was. Having never flown standby before and having no idea what he was talking about, I said, "Jesus." He was the only buddy I had in that moment. The man laughed and then proceeded to tell me that to fly standby, I needed to have a friend who worked for the airline.

We talked for a little while, and I felt God's favor on that interaction. The man told me to go to the domestic office and see if I could buy a ticket there. When I walked there with suitcase in hand, they looked at me kind of funny and could not believe I had just showed up at the airport without a ticket. I learned it would have been even more expensive to buy the ticket at the airport, so I decided to try knocking on a few more doors. I went to counter after counter to see if I could find favor or a cheap ticket, but I was not getting anywhere.

After a while of this, my friends and I sat down. I was at the end of my rope, and I was not sure what to do next. I felt as if I had filled my six water pots full of water and I was standing there, waiting for Jesus to turn all my efforts into wine. I had put myself out there. I was vulnerable. And I had people watching me. I needed a break from all this hoping and believing for the impossible. I needed to get some air and breathing room to figure out what to do next, since I had exhausted all viable options.

I took a walk in the airport to try to clear my head. Then the following question popped into my mind: *What if I don't make it to the wedding?* When I entertained that thought, I literally felt a cloud of discouragement come over me. After trying every door I could think of without anything opening up, I started to believe the lies that this would not work out, even though I had originally felt God on it. Doubt, discouragement and sadness overcame me in an instant. I had lived from my heart and was fully exposed, and now all hope was being shattered. When I put my eyes on the storm around me, my perspective shifted and I started to give up on this dream.

Have you ever been in a similar place, having taken a huge risk to be vulnerable to follow your heart, but then things just did not work out the way you hoped they would? I felt like something was dying inside of me. The discouragement and disappointment were making me never want to live from my heart again because it was just too painful. Thankfully, when I returned to where the others were sitting, they still had belief for this miracle. Their hope carried me, because by that point I had lost all hope. It is remarkable how we really do need family to lift us up when we are down. I am eternally grateful that Matt, Lisa and Brittany stayed with me and were there to encourage me when I needed it most.

We Need Family

I also decided to text some of my prayer warriors to intercede for a breakthrough. I told them that I was at the airport with no open doors and that I needed either $1,000, a buddy pass or to be transported to England. The deadline to get on a flight was approaching. I had to get on a flight that night or I would miss the wedding. My friends who were with me then asked if I knew anyone who worked for an airline. My friend Cristina Akers did, but the last time I had spoken with her, she was not able to help friends get cheap tickets, so it had not even crossed my mind to reach out to her. I decided to message her anyway. I had discipled Cristina more than a decade before and had even baptized her, and she had since become a good friend of mine. She lived in Colorado at the time and called me soon after I messaged her.

I followed the United man's suggestion and asked if she worked for them. She did not, but she did work for another airline that offered buddy passes, although she had never done one before. She asked me when I needed it. I told her within the next few hours. She was not sure if she could help, but she asked for my information and passport details.

As we were sitting on the bench in the airport, the same place where not long before I had told my friends they were free to explore the city but that I was not going to leave until I got on a flight, something in the atmosphere began to shift. Within moments Cristina found a flight, but it was leaving soon and I would have to get there as quickly as possible. The whole environment began to change suddenly. It became like a scene in a movie. My friends grabbed my luggage, and we began to run through the airport to find the airline in time.

When we made it to the airline kiosk, and while still on the phone with Cristina, I typed in my information on the check-in computer. My name appeared on the screen, and out popped a ticket from San Francisco to London! I could barely believe it! God did not let me down. The presence of God fell in a powerful way in that moment, and we all celebrated together. It was a true and unique miracle that I will remember for the rest of my life.

Cristina ended up getting my ticket for only $578. This was wonderful, just one-third of the price of a normal ticket and only $78 more than what I then had. Such great favor from the Lord! After getting checked in, while I was still at the airport, a friend told me he was nearby and wanted to come and say good-bye. He showed up and said he had it in his heart to give me money while in Redding, but he had not had the chance. We walked over to an ATM, and he gave me another $200! My ticket was completely paid for by that point, and I even had a little extra spending money for the journey.

I boarded the flight wearing the biggest smile of my life! As if that was not enough, I was blessed to have a friend hear of my overnight layover in Chicago who arranged for one of his friends to let me stay at her home. Right when I landed, I received a text from this precious sister, whom I had never met, saying that she had driven an hour to pick me up and give me a place to sleep for a few hours. The nice man sitting next to me, who had already heard all about my testimony of getting on the flight, was shocked at God's goodness and, I hope, inspired to learn more about the true and living God after hearing what He had done. When I arrived in London, I was incredibly blessed when friends who had driven more than an hour from Birmingham picked me up late that night. God is so good! And I love how He provides through family!

After a great night's sleep at my friend's house, I had the incredible privilege, honor and blessing to celebrate with the beautiful couple at their wedding. And the story does not end there. After the wedding I had the opportunity to go to Wales to re-dig the wells of the Welsh revival. A few of my friends from the Destiny House family happened to be there at that same time, so we met up and were able to tour the Bible College of Wales in Swansea, founded by Rees Howells, and then go to Loughor to visit the Moriah Chapel, which was significant to the beginning of the revival. I even got to sleep in the same house that Evan Roberts was born in and had his season of heavenly encounters. The trip to Wales was an added bonus to an already incredible and miraculous trip. The crazy thing is that while I was in England, a few precious friends sowed into my life, and I came back with more money than I had left with. God is good!

I am thankful to God for this miracle of turning water into wine on behalf of bringing the family of God together for such a special time. I love how Jesus' very first miracle in the Bible was when He turned water into wine at a wedding celebration. It goes to show how much He loves to celebrate life and bring family together in miraculous ways. I am thankful for how God came through above and beyond for me by using the beautiful Body of Christ, who surrounded me and believed with me for this miracle. May God receive all honor and glory for this miraculous gift!

Stepping into the Impossible Today

I share this testimony with you not so that you will show up at airports with bags packed and no ticket, but so that you will respond to the leading of the Holy Spirit to step out in faith toward the impossibilities He leads you to. As you follow your heart toward those things, including closed doors, trust in Him. He will empower you to walk on water. He will bring you into greater measures of His abundant life as you keep your focus on Him and open up your heart to receive from the Body of Christ.

I also want to make sure to say that while God broke through in a marvelous way this time, I also have many other stories of knocking on doors and nothing opening up. Many people asked me why I did not save up for this trip. Some people had trouble celebrating this miracle with me because it so confounded them. There are plenty of other times in my life when I was able to save up and actually buy plane tickets through the Lord's provision. But in the season I was in at that time, saving up was just not one of the options. God works differently in every time. The main thing is to be close to Him and to step out to risk as He leads.

Another important thing to notice in this breakthrough is that God did a miracle on my behalf not for a mission trip or some other ministry event, but simply to be with friends and family. He did this miracle because He loves relationships. The miraculous is not limited to healing the sick and raising the dead. These are incredible and important, but there are also times when God wants to do miracles on our behalf simply because He is in love with us and enjoys giving us the desires of our hearts. Peter walked on water not because someone's life depended on it, but solely because he had passion to be closer to Jesus.

The other crucial thing to notice here is that this miracle could not have happened without my brothers and sisters in Christ. I literally needed them all throughout the journey. There was a time when I had given up hope for this miracle, but my friends encouraged me. Others sowed into my trip in different ways, and still others covered me in prayer. The family of God partnered together in what God was doing and got to co-labor with Him in bringing the miracle to pass. We need each other to be launched into the fullness of our destinies. We cannot do it alone.

I pray that my testimony will inspire you to follow the leading of the Holy Spirit regardless of the surrounding circumstances and also to see the importance of inviting community into your risk taking. As you step out in faith to follow your heart and to seek Him first, even along unfamiliar paths, may He make a way where there is no way and enable you to walk on water, knitting you closer together with the Body of Christ in the process.

ACTIVATION: **We Need Each Other**

We really do need each other to step into the fullness of our destinies. I could not have made this journey without many others in the family of God partnering along the way.

1. From the list of twelve people you wrote out in chapter 8, whom of those can you reach out to and invite to partner with you as you step out in faith toward your destiny?

2. What can you do to deepen your relationships with those who matter most to you? And how can you

communicate your need for them rather than trying
to do it all by yourself?

3. In reading this testimony, what has the Lord stirred up
   inside of you?

4. Where in your life do you feel the Lord leading but it
   seems too impossible to even try?

   Maybe the Lord put that dream in your heart. Maybe
the impossible circumstances currently in your life exist
so that you can learn to rely more on God and the Body
of Christ. Maybe God wants to bless you so ridiculously
that He alone can receive all the credit. If He did not
even spare His own Son, how could He not also, along
with Him, give us all things? (See Romans 8:32.) God
loves to love us. He has the power and authority to enable you to walk on water as you move toward Him.

   May you receive a fresh impartation of faith today to
believe that what God has initiated, He will indeed bring
to pass regardless of the surrounding circumstances
(Philippians 1:6). I pray that as you keep your eyes on
Jesus and step out in faith toward the promises He has
given you, you will link arms with your brothers and
sisters in Christ to go even further in Him. May you
walk in new levels of intimacy with Jesus and with those
close to you and together enjoy the rich inheritance in
the Promised Land that He has destined for you.

> And I pray that you, being rooted and established in
> love, may have power, together with all the saints, to
> grasp how wide and long and high and deep is the
> love of Christ, and to know this love that surpasses
> knowledge—that you may be filled to the measure
> of all the fullness of God.

Now to him who is able to do immeasurably more than all we ask or imagine, according to his power that is at work within us, to him be glory in the church and in Christ Jesus throughout all generations, for ever and ever! Amen.

Ephesians 3:17–21

14

Hunger

No matter what Peter had already seen or experienced in his relationship with Jesus, he remained hungry for more. He pursued Jesus wholeheartedly and with reckless abandon. Once he was able to recognize Jesus, whether in the midst of a storm or after His resurrection, he was not afraid to get out of the boat again and again if Jesus was there waiting for him.

Boat Jumping, Take Two

In John 21, the disciples continued to ponder what their new life would look like after Jesus had been raised from the dead. Not many days following their interaction with the resurrected Lord, Peter decided to go fishing in the Sea of Tiberias. Some of the other disciples followed his lead. After a whole night of catching not even one fish, a Man appeared on the shore and told them to throw their nets on the right side of the boat. When they did what He told them to, they caught so many fish they were not able to haul the net in, 153 to be exact. When this happened, John realized that the Man on shore who had led them to their breakthrough was Jesus.

> As soon as Simon Peter heard [John] say, "It is the Lord," he wrapped his outer garment around him (for he had taken it off) and jumped into the water. The other disciples followed in the boat, towing the net full of fish, for they were not far from shore, about a hundred yards.
>
> John 21:7–8

The moment Peter recognized that it was Jesus, he jumped out of the boat! Sound familiar? There is something profound in this account. The hunger Peter demonstrated throughout his life is powerful. He just had to be near his friend Jesus. Whether that meant venturing to walk on water in the midst of a raging storm or jumping out of a boat to swim to shore, Peter's heart led him to Jesus every time. It did not matter how many radical encounters with Jesus Peter had had in the past. Though he had walked on water, was present at the Transfiguration and at the Garden of Gethsemane and had experienced miracle after miracle, every time he saw Jesus, he was compelled to draw closer. He was marked by the love of Jesus and wrecked for anything less.

Peter jumped out of the boat to be closer to Jesus more than once. He knew how to surrender and let go. Whenever Jesus showed up, it did not matter what Peter was holding on to for safety; he gladly and immediately risked it all to be closer to Him. It is not just one encounter we need with Jesus; we need a lifestyle, day after day, of doing life together with Him.

Not Just One Encounter

When Peter met Jesus for the first time, he had a significant encounter. After he was chosen as a disciple, his relationship grew and his encounters with Jesus increased. There were multiple defining moments that marked Peter's life in addition to walking on water. But Peter did not necessarily seek an experience or an encounter with Jesus; he sought Jesus Himself.

Meeting Jesus for the first time must have been amazing. Being at the Transfiguration must have been awesome, too. These and other interactions, however, were just invitations to a life full of adventure with Him and deeper intimacy. Peter never settled for or was satisfied with just one profound encounter with Jesus. Once he met Jesus, he was captivated for life. Peter was willing to follow Jesus wherever He might go, even if that meant walking on water in the middle of a storm. Peter had experienced the love of Jesus and was ruined for anything else. Where else could he go from there? He was so in love with Jesus that his lifestyle was defined by leaving everything behind to run to Jesus whenever He showed up.

Encounters with Jesus are beautiful. But we should never seek an encounter just to have some ecstatic experience. Our desire should always be to grow closer to Jesus and to become one with Him. If miracles are birthed from that union, that is wonderful. If nothing is produced other than a deepening of love, that is just as significant. Falling in love knows no bounds.

We can learn from Peter's story the importance of becoming aware of the presence of Jesus and immediately responding to draw near. No matter how many times we see Jesus do the impossible on our behalf, encounter us with His love, give us divine revelations or heal us, He wants our hunger for Him to increase. He wants us to recognize Him in those moments when He manifests His presence. He longs for us to respond by dropping everything to be with Him.

When God crashes into our day, do we stop everything to draw near to the One who has manifested Himself in a greater way? When He actually comes and reveals Himself in a greater measure, can we let everything go simply to remain in Him?

Apprehended at the Home of Peace

I remember a defining moment in 2014 when I learned the importance of yielding to God's presence. When I was hosting a group of leaders from Bethel School of Supernatural Ministry for a retreat at the Home of Peace in Oakland, I felt God show up in a powerful way when I was not expecting it. A few of us were worshiping in the chapel around the time I was supposed to give the group a tour of the house. The presence of God was so powerful in the chapel that I did not want to leave. I also did not want to let down one of my spiritual fathers, who had organized the retreat. Do I follow through with the original plan to give them a tour of the house, or do I let everything go and remain in Him in that moment? I am a very responsible person, and I value my commitments to build trust and stay true to my integrity. I struggled with what to do and was forced to make a decision.

Having spent my whole life asking for more of God, I could not bring myself to tell God to wait while I went to my other commitment. Can you imagine me saying, "God, excuse me. I know You are here right now and that You want to speak to me and touch my heart in a profound way, but I have another appointment. Would You mind waiting here while I do that, and then I will return to commune with You afterward?" No way! God must have priority in our lives and over our plans. We need both to be intentional to make plans to be with Him and also to yield and allow Him to interrupt our schedules when He shows up in a significant way. In that moment, I decided to yield and stay where I felt Him powerfully. In the end, the group figured out a way to tour the house and then joined us in the chapel, where we had a great time continuing to commune with God together.

I learned that when God's presence manifests in an intensified way or when I feel the power of God increase in a moment, I need to stop and yield. If my regular prayers are for Him to meet me in greater measures, then when He does this, I need to be willing to receive, no matter what the hour.

Insatiable Hunger

One of my personal heroes, one who has inspired my life and taken my faith to new levels, is Carrie Judd Montgomery, the founder of the Home of Peace. She remained hungry for the Lord throughout her entire life, no matter what experiences she had already had with Him. She has an incredible story of being healed miraculously and then starting some of the earliest healing homes in the country in her early twenties. She later was baptized in the Spirit at the age of fifty and had other personal and profound encounters with the Lord. But even after all these encounters Carrie did not cease to hunger for more of the Lord. Even with her ministry successes, she understood the importance of remaining in the Lord on a daily basis. When she was more than fifty years old, she wrote about continuing to encounter Jesus in even greater measures in an article entitled "The Life on Wings: The Possibilities of Pentecost." I share an excerpt below because I believe it will stir up deeper hunger inside of you to press in for more of His presence today.

Early this morning as the power of God was upon me, and I was recognizing, as I so often love to do, the presence of the indwelling Comforter, and worshipping Him in His temple, with the Father and the Son, was led out in prayer for different things, but all at once He said to me, "I want you to recognize definitely that I am filling the temple." Of course, I know He always fills it, but this was something a little different and He wanted the recognition that every part of spirit, soul and body was pervaded with His presence, and that meant, as He revealed to me His meaning, that I should drop even prayer for the time and be occupied with the presence of His glory, and I said, "Oh, God, the Holy Ghost, Thou art filling Thy temple," and immediately, just as though a little vial of attar of roses had been broken in this room and every part of it would soon be filled with the perfume, so the presence of His glory, sensibly pervaded every part of my being and even love and prayer were lost in worship. Then I thought of the time in the Old Testament when the temple was so filled with God's glory that the priest could not even stand to minister.

There is, therefore, an experience beyond service and beyond prayer, and that is a revelation of His own personality to such an extent that there is nothing but adoring worship filling our being. Usually it is a blessed experience to be able to speak in tongues, to let the heavenly song flow out, but there are times when even tongues cease, when His presence is so all-pervading and the atmosphere so heavenly that I cannot talk at all in any language, but the power of His blessed Spirit upon me is so marvelous that it seems as though I were almost dwelling in heaven.

I hope this testimony will make some one press on for the fulness. The Word tells us, "That the communication of thy faith may become effectual by the acknowledging of every good thing which is in you in Christ Jesus." Philemon 6. Through our faithful testimony somebody else's torch may be lighted in the love and providence of God, and suppose we should hesitate for fear of persecution, should stop acknowledging every good thing which is in us in Christ Jesus, and somebody's torch should fail to be lit. We have a great responsibility, and if we fail in testimony our own light will grow dim. . . .

In Psalm 103:5, we read, "Who satisfieth thy mouth with good things; so that thy youth is renewed like the eagle's." Here is a reference to the eagle again, the youth renewed like the eagle's. Beloved, I do not believe in growing old, do you? I believe God means just what He says. Isn't it beautiful? I never expect to grow old. The years may slip over my head, but what of that? That has nothing to do with it. He who has eternal youth is my youth and my strength.

Now, who is going to trust God for the winged life? You can crawl instead if you wish. God will even bless you if you crawl; He will do the best He can for you, but oh how much better to avail ourselves of our wonderful privileges in Christ and to "mount up with wings as eagles, run and not be weary, walk and not faint." O beloved friends, there is a life on wings. I feel the streams of His life fill me and permeate my mortal frame from my head to my feet, until no words are adequate to describe it. I can only make a few bungling attempts to tell you what it is like and ask the Lord to reveal to you the rest. May He reveal to you your inheritance in Christ Jesus so that you will press on and get all that He has for you.[1]

ACTIVATION: Cultivating Hunger

Healing revivalist Smith Wigglesworth once said, "I would rather have a man on my platform not filled with the Holy Ghost but hungry for God, than a man who has received the Holy Ghost but has become satisfied with his experience."[2] Hunger is powerful. There is no growth without it. In Matthew 5:6, Jesus said, "Blessed are those who hunger and thirst for righteousness, for they will be filled."

Have you been around people who are hungry for Jesus lately? Do you know people who are desperate for more of Jesus at any cost, who have already experienced a great measure of His love yet are still poor in spirit and realize their utter dependence upon Him? These people are contagious. They stir up hunger in me like nothing else. I do not ever want to be completely satisfied—there is always more of Jesus to know. I want to have a healthy balance of extreme gratitude and thankfulness alongside extreme poverty of spirit and hunger for more of the Lord.

Just as we see in Peter's life, one of the common threads in the lives of the revivalists I have studied is an insatiable hunger for more of God. These saints and heroes make time to get away and feast on the presence of God, and they also allow Him to interrupt their schedules. All throughout Scripture, the prophets of old, the disciples and the saints we celebrate each had this deep inner life. They cultivated hunger throughout their lives.

1. I want to ask you today: How can you remain hungry and cultivate more hunger in your own life? Have you considered fasting as a good place to start?[3]

2. When you think of someone with a deep hunger for God, who comes to mind?

   Being around hungry people will make you hungrier for God. How can you position yourself to do life more consistently with those who burn for Jesus and are hungry for more of Him?

3. I encourage you this week to initiate a regular time in worship and prayer with one or more of the people God has highlighted. Watch to see what the Lord does

in your life and how He increases hunger deep within
you.

Holy Spirit, make us hungry for more of You. Jesus, we
want only You. Father, draw us near today. It is You who
puts that hunger in our hearts for more. So we welcome
that hunger in our lives today. We make space for You
to come however You want to fill us today. Come, Holy
Spirit, and have Your way. Make us desperate for You like
never before. Let nothing else satisfy but the life-giving
love that comes from Jesus. All our love is for You.

15

Obsession

There I sat, all alone, facing the piano in the chapel at the Home of Peace. It was the summer of 2015, and I was in the midst of another storm. I had risked my heart and become vulnerable, and the "ground" beneath me was shaky. I had no idea what was going to happen next. My future and a potentially significant relationship were up in the air, and I did not know where I was going to land. If things did not turn out like I had imagined, it would mean starting all over again. I felt like I had heard God speak loud and clear. That was the only reason I had unveiled my heart to go all in. Was I wrong? What was I to make of all the signs I felt He had given me? It was one of those moments when I had absolutely no control and was utterly dependent on Jesus. I was trying my best to surrender all and to trust in Him no matter what might come. I was praying for His fire to come and refine my heart even though I knew it could be painful.

All I could do was attempt to put all my trust in Him and focus my attention on Jesus rather than on the "what ifs" I was facing. I played the piano and just worshiped. When I did, my heart's cry came out in this melody.

> I will remain in You
> You are my anchor still
> I will remain in You
> You are my anchor still
> My anchor still
> My anchor still
>
> I'll put my hope in You
> How You hold me still
> I'll put my hope in You
> How You hold me still
> You hold me still
> Come hold me still

My tender heart was poured out to the Lord in that little chapel. I felt that I had followed my heart into the middle of turbulent waters. The safety of the boat was too far behind me now. The only option I had was to cling to Jesus and to trust in Him. There was no going back; I had ventured too far into this sea to turn around. This song was my declaration that no matter what storms may come and disrupt my expectations, break my heart or strip me bare, I was making a choice to remain in Him. I would keep my eyes fixed on Him, whatever may come.

Anchor Still

God alone is my anchor and my safe place. He alone is my refuge. He is the One to whom I can run in the midst of the storms. He is my only hope. I was determined that I would remain in Him. Whether or not circumstances turned out to be what I expected, I would be safe in Him. I could trust that He is in control and knows what is best for me. Even though I might not have necessarily felt these things in that moment of my life, singing this song was my declaration of faith that I was going to remain in Him no matter what.

I ended up making it through that storm and was very thankful for where all the pieces fell in the end. My faith was strengthened even more in the knowledge that God is for me and with me. I experienced His love in that He wants the very best for me and for others, and that He will never let me compromise for anything less than His best. In retrospect, I was grateful for His protection and covering over my life in that moment of surrender. The pain of shattered dreams and expectations was real. I had to take time to process and grieve the disappointment and loss. I was confused and disillusioned. It took some time for hope to be restored in that area of my heart. In that season, He held me still. The level of trust I have in my Father only deepened in that moment, for which I am forever grateful.

Nearly a year after that time at the Home of Peace, I found myself again sitting in front of a piano, this time in the upper room at Destiny House during our annual week of prayer and fasting. Every morning during our fasting week, some of us who lived together met to worship and adore Jesus, wait on Him, listen and pray. This particular morning with just a few of us gathered, I played the piano spontaneously as our hearts burned together for more of Jesus. I ended up playing the "Anchor Still" song that I had written the year before in my fragile state.

At the end of our worship and prayer time, I began to read and declare John 15 over our community and our future season together. As I was reading it, I came to John 15:4, where Jesus says, "Remain in me, and I will remain in you." In that moment, I began to see the pieces come together. The line in John 15, "I will remain in you," was the same line in the song I had written a year before and that we had just sung.

When I originally birthed that song, the themes in my mind were more connected with the word *still*: Be *still* and know that I am God (Psalm 46:10); He is my anchor *still* throughout all the storms and heartaches; He remains faithful through all circumstances of life. When I sang this song in a new season and read John 15 afterward, the phrase *I will remain in You* jumped out. Even though the song was not based on John 15, I had been declaring it through the words of the song without even realizing it. God formed and birthed something in my heart in the midst of clinging to Him in a storm that would reveal more of His heart for our community a year later. I am always undone and blown away by the layers of God's goodness, revealed to us again and again.

Remain in Me

Jesus wants us to remain in Him and to draw even closer to His heart. He wants to become one with us. It is not just about one face-to-face encounter that will sustain us for the next twenty years. Yes, that encounter can and will mark us for life, but encounters are only the beginning, entryways into even greater levels of intimacy with Jesus. Intimacy is diving even deeper into the limitless oceans of His love. We must remain in Him on a daily basis to live the abundant life that He died for us to have. Our lives should be one long encounter with the living God, always connected to our Source.

John 15 describes Jesus as the true vine and His Father as the gardener who cuts off unfruitful branches and prunes good ones so they become even more fruitful. Jesus said in verses 4–5,

Remain in me, and I will remain in you. No branch can bear
fruit by itself; it must remain in the vine. Neither can you
bear fruit unless you remain in me. I am the vine; you are the
branches. If a man remains in me and I in him, he will bear
much fruit; apart from me you can do nothing.

If I remain in Him, He promises to remain in me. Now, that
is powerful! Not only that, but He promises to bear much
fruit in and through my life. And the truest part of it all is
that I can do nothing apart from Him. I do not ever want to
minister or lead a meeting or host a worship night apart from
Him. He is the reason we gather. He is the reason I speak.
He is the reason I write. It is all in and through and for Him.
If His presence does not come and rest upon the people, it is
just a nice little sermon. If people do not encounter the love
and presence of God in the books I write, what is the point?
Nothing else really matters to me besides Jesus. All I want
is for the overshadowing presence of God to come and fill
and mark people with the love of Jesus like never before. I
want the name of Jesus to be lifted high. I want Him to be
honored and loved well. I want to affect God's heart with
burning passion and love. I want my heart to burn for Him. I
want to become one with Him. This kind of love and passion
is displayed beautifully in Song of Solomon 8:6–7:

Place me like a seal over your heart, like a seal on your arm;
for love is as strong as death, its jealousy unyielding as the
grave. It burns like blazing fire, like a mighty flame. Many
waters cannot quench love; rivers cannot wash it away. If one
were to give all the wealth of his house for love, it would be
utterly scorned.

The best way to bear fruit, to change the world and to
step into the impossible is simply to fall more in love with

Jesus each day. It is that place of intimacy and remaining in Him that allows us to bear fruit that will last. We have absolutely nothing without Him. He is our Source. He is our life. He is our love.

And My Heart Burns

All God wants from us is passion. Peter had hunger and passion for Jesus. It made him do ridiculous, uncontrollable, impulsive acts to get closer to Jesus when none of it made sense. Peter had to remain close to Jesus. He was completely lost without Him. In a time when many of His followers totally abandoned Him, Jesus asked His twelve disciples, "You do not want to leave too, do you?" Simon Peter answered him, "Lord, to whom shall we go? You have the words of eternal life" (John 6:67–68).

From the beginning, Peter had nowhere else to go. He was all in. No turning back. Jesus had won his heart. Who else could fully satisfy like Jesus? Who else could make every cell in his body come alive like never before? Who else could inspire him to live fully from his heart to become the person he was created to be? Who else could give him purpose and a destiny? Who else could accept him exactly the way he was and make him feel this loved? It was Jesus. Jesus, Jesus, Jesus. Only Jesus. No one could ever mark him like Jesus. Everything inside of him came alive at the sight of Jesus. Compelling love has no bounds. Just one taste and he was captivated for life. No going back.

Jesus, the all-powerful, humble King. Jesus, the One who loves us through our shame. Jesus, the One who sees, understands and knows us like no one else ever could. Jesus, the One who never abandons us, never forsakes us and never leaves us. Jesus, the One who remains with us when all else fails. Jesus, the One who lived to die just for us. Jesus, the most passionate love revolutionary to ever walk the earth. It is Jesus, the all-consuming fire, the One who causes every vein in our bodies to be filled with passion and to come alive and burn for Him. Jesus, Jesus, Jesus. No other can ever compare. No other love will ever satisfy. No other lover can touch us in the deepest places like He can. No one else is as trustworthy, safe or faithful. It is Jesus, the ever-present help in time of need. Jesus, the One who will always make time to be with us. It is Jesus, Jesus, Jesus. The only One worthy of all our praise.

ACTIVATION: **Adoration to Jesus**

In light of His goodness, let's just worship Jesus right now. Let a song be poured out as a love offering to Him. Let the only purpose of your worship in this moment be to lavish love upon Him. Let's thank Him for who He is, celebrate His goodness and lift His name on high.

> Jesus, You are the all-powerful and intimate friend. You are kind and compassionate. You are the humble King. Jesus, we adore You. No one else in this world can ever compare with You. You are our Rock and our fortress. You are our safe place. You are our hope and our light in the dark places. Jesus, You are burning love. You are kind and gracious to us. We adore You, Jesus. There is no one else we love or desire as much as You. No one else can compare. Our lives are for You.
>
> You have our yes. No matter what it looks like, no matter what the cost, we say yes to You, Jesus. Have Your way in our hearts. Whatever it takes to be closer to You, we say yes. We will leave the safety and comfort of our boats and step into the

midst of the storm if You are there. We will go into the darkest places of this world and into the painful places in others' hearts to bring Your love. Whatever it looks like, we do not care. We just want more of You. We must have more of You. We cannot go on another day without more of You. We cannot even take another breath without You. You are the vine, and we are the branches. You are our life source.

Come and overshadow us today in Your glory. Come and invade and take over our lives. We offer You total abandonment and surrender, and we ask that You would come and possess us fully. Teach us how to love You more, Lord. Let us be led by our hearts that have been captivated by Your love. We are all in. Jesus, our love is for You. Our lives are for You. You are welcome in every part of our hearts, Lord. We do not want just a visitation; we want a habitation. Come and make Yourself at home. Let our lives become resting places for You to dwell. Come and burn in us an unquenchable passion for You like never before. Jesus, Jesus, Jesus, there is no one quite like You. Meet us just as You want to. We love You. Our lives are for You.

16

Courage

Experiencing a life of miracles comes down to falling more in love with Jesus. Stepping into the impossible happens differently every time and comes from a place of relationship, not principle. There is no "how to" in relation to stepping into the impossible. Miracles happen as we keep our eyes fixed on Jesus and go on a journey of intimacy with Him. At the end of our lives—at the end of it all—it is all about becoming one with God and remaining in Him.

Just as a husband and wife come together in moments of greater intimacy, the two becoming one, we, too, share intimate moments with God. In addition to significant encounters we have with Him in various seasons, we also do normal life with Him. All of this builds our relationship with Him.

When I ponder how we can position ourselves to fall more in love with Jesus, it makes me think of how a woman falls in love with the man of her dreams, or vice versa. Falling in love with Jesus will look different for every person, and there will come a time when choosing love becomes vital. The things that will always deepen and strengthen our relationship with Him, however, are the investment of time and an open heart. Vulnerability in sharing hearts in any relationship is life-giving and nurtures a growing relationship. To share our innermost feelings with God and with each other takes great courage. The word *courage* we use today comes from the Latin root word *cor*, which means "heart."[1] Courage is simply bravery to live from the depths of our hearts.

Reading the Bible, praying, fasting, silence, worship and community are all pillars of keeping the fire of our love for God burning. It also helps to be around others whose flames are burning passionately for Jesus and who can stoke the fire when our flames are burning dim. We can do all of these things to position ourselves to grow closer to Him, but we also need courage to be vulnerable and to share our hearts. We need to let Him into the hidden cracks and recesses of our hearts as we engage in these graces to draw near. We need to let Him love us in the deepest places. We need to open wide our hearts to receive His unfailing love.

The initial falling in love with Jesus is only the beginning. It is the mature growing in and choosing love over time that sustains a healthy relationship. We need to stay close to the Flame that is greater than any other to keep the fire for God burning within our hearts.

Intimacy and Risk

Taking risks and following our hearts outside of intimacy with Jesus is dangerous. If we do this, we may still see the impossible, but it may not be coming from His heart. Walking in the miraculous should never be divorced from intimacy with Jesus. Breakthroughs are empty without Him. Eternal value comes from the One who is our Source of life.

In Matthew 7:21–23, Jesus warns against doing great miracles and stepping into the impossible apart from a heart connection with Him:

> Not everyone who says to me, "Lord, Lord," will enter the kingdom of heaven, but only he who does the will of my Father who is in heaven. Many will say to me on that day, "Lord, Lord, did we not prophesy in your name, and in your name drive out demons and perform many miracles?" Then I will tell them plainly, "I never knew you. Away from me, you evildoers!"

The people in the latter half of this passage hardly seem to me to be evildoers, with all their great deeds and miracles. Without relationship with Jesus, however, this life of miracles is dangerous and even harmful. In the beginning of this passage, it also says that those who call out to Him but who do not do His will will not get very far. Being close to Jesus without stepping out in faith can also be dangerous, because He longs for us to demonstrate His love to a lost and dying world. Both knowing Jesus but not doing His will and not knowing Him but taking great risks to perform miracles are missing the target.

In light of these two extremes, can you imagine what kind of catalytic power might be released when you marry intimacy with Jesus and risk taking? What might happen when we step out in faith from a place of relationship with Jesus? I believe this is the perfect combination to position ourselves to step into the impossible. Signs, miracles and convergence naturally flow from a lifestyle of becoming one with Jesus and risk taking. When we are in love with Him, we gain courage to step out in faith as He leads, and we become unstoppable. Pure and devoted hearts gain wings to soar into unknown realms of glory and impossibilities.

If we want to step into the impossible on a more regular basis, we need to grow closer to Jesus and take risks. If we spend time with Him, we can then follow our hearts because they have been shaped by His desires in His presence. We gain courage to face impossible situations with great hope, promise and expectation for God to come through. Many times, following Jesus may lead us into dangerous places. But when He is near, that is always the safest place to be.

Courage of the Unschooled

As Peter grew in his relationship with Jesus, he also grew in greater courage to step into more signs and wonders. The courage Peter cultivated in the midst of the storm continued to develop as he took more risks. After Jesus' death, resurrection and ascension, Acts 3:1–8 says that Peter and John were going to the temple to pray when they came across a crippled beggar who sat in front of the temple each day. When this feeble man saw Peter and John, he asked them for money. He was desperate for deliverance and needed help. Peter "looked straight at him" and said to the man, "Look at us!" Peter knew about focus.

When Peter had his full attention, he said, "Silver or gold I do not have, but what I have I give to you. In the name of Jesus Christ of Nazareth, walk" (verse 6). Then Peter grabbed his right hand and helped him up. Instantly the man's feet and ankles became strong. Legs that had been crippled since birth were restored. What happened to this man was literally impossible. Atrophy would have long ago set in. It should have taken much more time to rebuild muscle and bone for him to be able to walk.

When this man's legs became strong, "he jumped to his feet and began to walk. Then he went with them into the temple courts, walking and jumping, and praising God" (verse 8). What a beautiful response from one who had lived in such a debilitating storm his whole life. The moment Peter had the courage to step into his circumstances to bring the power of Jesus, the man was totally healed, restored and made whole.

This man's miracle stirred up controversy and trouble in the town. The people got even more agitated when Peter boldly proclaimed that the source of the miracle came from the name of Jesus. The fire of revival began to spread, and nearly five thousand people were added to the Kingdom through Peter and John's ministry there. The religious officials did not like this at all, so they threw Peter and John in prison. The next day, they were questioned about what they had done. Filled with the Holy Spirit, Peter boldly responded that this miracle happened "by the name of Jesus Christ of Nazareth" (Acts 4:10), and then he called all of them to get saved.

Then, in Acts 4:13, it says, "When they saw the courage of Peter and John and realized that they were unschooled, ordinary men, they were astonished and they took note that these men had been with Jesus." I love how when the Jewish leaders saw the *courage* of Peter and John, they realized that the only explanation was that they *had been with Jesus*. The Greek word for *courage* used in this passage is *parrhesia*, which means "freedom, openness, boldness and confidence," especially as it relates to speech. It comes from the root word *pas*, which means "all."[2] Peter and John had no degrees, gold medals or worldly accomplishments to prove themselves. They were mere fishermen before they met Jesus, but they had access to the power of God and the miraculous because they were *all* in. They had friendship with Jesus, had spent time in His presence and lived from their hearts.

Spending time with Jesus was how they got the courage to bring deliverance to the crippled man and to speak boldly to the crowd. Peter had already experienced Jesus stilling the storm in his own heart and imparting courage to walk on water. Now it was time for him to partner with Jesus to bring peace and healing to others in the midst of their storms. The people were astonished. There was no other reason to explain the courage of these unschooled men other than the fact that they had been with Jesus.

Take Courage

I believe that the Lord is taking us into new realms with Him that will require greater levels of courage. There are increasing breakthroughs He wants us to step into, new lands He wants us to discover, vaster inheritances He wants us to possess and greater adventures He wants us to pioneer. We are about to go somewhere we have never been before (Joshua 3:3–4).

Stepping out into the unknown as Peter did requires courage. The first time Peter "stepped out of the boat" required courage, as did the second and third and fourth times. If we are continually moving forward with Jesus and bringing His love to the world, each time we step out requires a measure of courage.

If we want to grow in courage like Peter did, we need to spend time with Jesus and take more risks. We will likely face intimidation, fear of rejection, fear of failure, fear of man and so on. It is important to step out to love anyway. We have not been given a spirit of fear but of love and of a sound mind (2 Timothy 1:7). We need to follow what we think might be the leading of the Holy Spirit even if we are not 100 percent sure. We need to be bold to share our hearts. In the process of risking and following our hearts, we will grow in discernment in hearing the voice of the Lord.

Mary of Bethany stepped out in great courage to follow her heart when she poured out expensive perfume on Jesus (John 12:1–8; Mark 14:3–9). To do this she first had to overcome fear of man and not care what anyone else but Jesus thought. She also had to interrupt a meal Jesus was having with His closest friends. The disciples were offended by her actions and publicly rebuked her; Jesus, however, recognized her extravagant act of love and stood by her side to defend her.[3] Courage is not the absence of fear; it is the ability to live wholeheartedly regardless of any resistance (Isaiah 43). Just as He did with Mary, Jesus will also stand by our side when we seek to love Him with *all* of our hearts.

We do not need courage to do nothing. We only need courage if we are about to do something great or impossible. God commanded Joshua to be strong and courageous multiple times just before he was about to fight to take possession of the Promised Land. In Joshua 1:9, He said, "Have I not commanded you? Be strong and courageous. Do not be terrified; do not be discouraged, for the LORD your God will be with you wherever you go."

The Hebrew word used for *courage* here is *amats*, which can mean "strong, bold, steadfast, established, confirmed and determined."[4] In this verse we see that courage is not an option; it is a command. Jesus later said that if we love Him, we will keep His commands (John 14:15). We are actually commanded to be courageous. We are called by God to step out to take risks to follow His leading and to follow our hearts no matter what the surrounding circumstances look like. He calls us to walk in courage, not fear. Just as Jesus called out to Peter and the disciples in the boat, "Take courage! It is I. Don't be afraid" (Matthew 14:27), He is speaking the same to us today.

Jesus says, *Come*

Just as He was with Peter out on the dangerous waters, calling him to come and meet Him there, Jesus is entreating you today. He is calling you to be strong and courageous and to consecrate yourself, for "tomorrow the LORD will do amazing things among you" (Joshua 3:5). You have a choice today. What will you do with the seed of this book that has now been planted in you? Will you throw off every weight, concern, safety net and security to step outside of the boat to draw nearer to Him?

What would it look like if you let go of everything and all control, even just for a moment? What would your life look like if absolutely nothing, no one and no fear were holding you back today? What would happen if you were crazy in love with Jesus and did not care what anyone else thought of your wild passion? What would it look like to experience such love that you were ruined for anything less than wholehearted surrender? What would it look like to live freely from the depths of your heart without holding back?

Jesus has already paid the ultimate price because of love. He has already won our hearts. He has already given all of Himself for us. When we have Him, we have everything. He is the abundant life who satisfies like no other. Knowing Him is our truest destiny. He is always our answer. He is drawing us into total vulnerability, surrender and dependence on Him. He is calling us to live from the depths of our hearts where we are unafraid to step out to love.

Our lives are not our own; we were bought at a price. He is worth our yes. He is worth it all. He is worth leaving everything behind to cling to Him. He is calling us today to come. He is longing for us to join Him out there in the turbulent waters. His heart yearns for us to come near. He loves

180

us more than we can ever know. He is waiting for us to stop everything to just sit with Him for a while. He has secrets He wants to whisper in our ears. Jesus is at the door of our hearts, knocking so He can come in a little closer (Revelation 3:20). It is time to let our walls down. It is time to let Him love us through our pain. We can trust Him with our whole hearts.

It is no accident that you picked up *Walking on Water*. God is setting you apart to be a burning one for Him. He is shifting your life in ways that feel uncomfortable. The reason you feel the refining fire is because He is preparing you for more. He is about to expand your territory (Isaiah 54:1–5). He is calling you higher than you have ever gone before. He is imparting fresh hunger. He is drawing you to new levels of intimacy. He is stirring up passion and marking you with weightier holiness and consecration than ever before. He is commissioning you as a fearless lover who will go wherever He goes and love whomever He loves. He is waiting for you out on the waters. Take courage; now is your time to live from your heart and to step outside of the boat. His eyes will always guide you home.

ACTIVATION: Living from Your Heart

Are there any areas in your heart that you are withholding from God because they are too painful to expose? Are there people in your life you care deeply about who need to know how much you love and appreciate them? For your final activation, I want to challenge you to be courageous to share your heart beyond your previous limits.

1. Be more vulnerable with God than you have ever been before. Tell Him your innermost thoughts and feelings.

Invite Him into the deepest places of your heart. Allow Him to come into every room of your heart to love you even in the painful places. Be honest and vulnerable to share your disappointments and frustrations with Him. Let Him love you exactly where you are today. You can do this through journaling, prayer, silence or however you best connect with God. The main thing here is to be as honest as you possibly can, the good, the bad and the ugly, and to sit with God even if it is uncomfortable and allow Him to love you through. His love covers even the darkest places (Romans 8:38–39).

2. Proverbs 27:5 says, "Better is open rebuke than hidden love." Wow! How many people do you have in your life that you secretly love? In other words, do these people you love actually know how much you care about them? Now is your chance to tell people how special they are to you and why they mean that much to you. It takes great courage to be vulnerable to express your heart and to encourage others. Do not limit this activation to only one person. Maybe there are several people on your heart that you really love and need to show that to this week. Write an encouraging note. Send flowers. Cook a meal. Call someone up simply to say, "I love you." Have fun with this. Watch and see what happens as you courageously demonstrate love to those who matter most.

17

Burn

Thank you for joining me on this adventure in *Walking on Water*. It has been an honor to be a part of what God is doing in and through your life. I would love to hear testimonies of what has happened in you as a result of reading this book. I hope to meet you in person one day so we can celebrate the goodness of God together. And now, as we end this journey to begin a new one . . .

I pray that God would seal what has been released in your life and that His love would cover every promise that has been deposited in your heart. May your healing be complete, and may you find your tribe of burning ones to run with. I pray for fruit that remains, fire that burns brighter and faith to step into the impossible. I pray that you become a target for the love of the Father like never before and that you are mantled with great courage, knowing He is with you always.

I pray that your focus never leaves the face of Jesus. I bless you with a fierce determination to take hold of Him no matter what the cost. May you be marked by His presence all the days of your life. May you be ruined for anything less than His satisfying love. I bless you with a life that cannot function or exist without His presence. I pray that you are undone by the one thing and that Psalm 27 becomes a new anthem in your life. I pray that you would burn with a fiery passion and fall deeper in love with Jesus each day. May you receive a fresh impartation of hunger for God. May the Holy Spirit continue to come in even greater power for His name's sake. I bless you with a mighty baptism of the love and the fire of God. May you be utterly swept away in the tender love of Jesus until you are willing to go anywhere and do anything to be closer to Him still.

Jesus, without You, we have nothing. But with You, we have everything. You are our one thing. You are the reason we move and breathe and have our being. You are our hope. You are always the answer. You are Lord above all storms. You are the source of courageous faith to step into the impossible. You are the One who does miracles. You are the most intimate lover we could ever know. You are the truest love revolutionary to ever exist. No one else satisfies like You. No one else loves us the way You do. We only want You. No matter what the cost, we say yes to loving You with our whole hearts, because You have already paid the greatest price. You are worth it all. Our lives are for You.

And finally, my friend, no matter what storms may come your way, I charge you to always

> Turn your eyes upon Jesus
> Look full in His wonderful face
> And the things of earth will grow strangely dim
> In the light of His glory and grace[5]

184

Notes

Chapter 3: Peace in the Storm

1. John 6:19 says that they had rowed about three and a half miles before Jesus came to them. They were literally right in the middle of the sea by that time, struggling and alone.

2. The word translated "against" is the Greek word *enantios*, which is a combination of *en* + *antios*. *Antios* means "set against," and *en* ("in") heightens and intensifies the meaning of the word.

3. *New Testament Lexicon*, trans. and rev. Joseph H. Thayer (New York: Harper & Brothers, 1889), s.v. "basanizo," http://biblehub.com/greek/928.htm.

4. Resistance is a combination of *re-* ("against") and *sistere* ("take a stand, stand firm"; similar to the word *assist*).

5. Online Parallel Bible Project, "5015. tarassó," Bible Hub, accessed March 10, 2017, http://biblehub.com/greek/5015.htm. *Tarasso* can also mean "to get too stirred up inside, to take away calmness of mind, and to make restless."

6. Percy Livingstone Parker, ed., *The Heart of John Wesley's Journal* (London: Fleming H. Revell Company, 1903), 6–8.

Chapter 4: The Art of Letting Go

1. Jeanne Guyon, *Experiencing the Depths of Jesus Christ* (Jacksonville, Fla.: SeedSowers, 1975), 33.

2. Miriam Huffman Rockness, *A Passion for the Impossible: The Life of Lilias Trotter* (Grand Rapids, Mich.: Discovery House, 1999), 91.

3. Jennifer A. Miskov, *Life on Wings: The Possibilities of Pentecost* (Cleveland, Tenn.: CPT Press, 2012), 7–23, 35–45. To learn more about the Home of Peace or to visit, see www.homeofpeace.com.

4. Bill Johnson with Jennifer A. Miskov, *Defining Moments: God-Encounters with Ordinary People Who Changed the World* (New Kensington, Pa.: Whitaker House, 2016), 267–291.

5. Norman Grubb, *Rees Howells, Intercessor: The Story of a Life Lived for God* (Fort Washington, Pa.: Christian Literature Crusade, 1952), 35. Howells said of this experience, "It never dawned on me before that the Holy Ghost was a Person exactly like the Savior, and that He must come and dwell in flesh and blood. . . . I had only thought of Him as an Influence coming on meetings, and that was what most of us in the Revival thought. I had never seen that He must live in bodies, as the Savior lived in His on earth."

6. Ibid., 36–37.

7. Ibid., 38.

8. Ibid. See also Doris M. Ruscoe, *The Intercession of Rees Howells* (Blowing Rock, N.C.: Zerubbabel Press, 1983), 43–44.

9. Ruscoe, *Intercession*, 42–43.

10. Ibid.

11. Grubb, *Rees Howells*, 39.

12. Ibid.

13. Ibid., 114. See also Ruscoe, *Intercession*, 44.

14. Grubb, *Rees Howells*, 119.

15. Ibid., 100.

16. Ibid., 185–187.

17. Ibid., 217.

18. Ibid., 218–219, 221.

19. Ibid.; see also David Littlewood, "Rees Howells," *The Remnant International*, July 2000, http://www.theremnant.com/07-06-00.html.

Chapter 6: Focus

1. *Focus* was "taken by Kepler (1604) in a mathematical sense for 'point of convergence,' perhaps on analogy of the burning point of a lens." Douglas Harper, Online Etymology Dictionary, accessed March 20, 2017, http://www.etymonline.com/index.php?term=focus. This meaning can also be seen in its synonyms: *center, heart, core, nucleus, point of convergence.*

2. *Hearth* can mean the floor in front of a fireplace or the lowest part of a furnace, where ore or metal is exposed to the flame. Once the metal or gold is exposed here, it is softened and able to be molded into something new.

3. Exodus 14:15–18 and Joshua 7:10–15 are two examples of when the Lord called Moses and Joshua to take action instead of just crying out before Him.

4. See Jennifer A. Miskov with Heidi Baker, Lou Engle, and Bill Johnson, *Ignite Azusa: Positioning for a New Jesus Revolution* (Redding, Calif.: Silver to Gold, 2016), 45.

5. Frank Bartleman, *How Pentecost Came to Los Angeles: As It Was in the Beginning*, 2nd ed. (Los Angeles: Frank Bartleman, 1925), 39; now available at Frank Bartleman, *How Pentecost Came to Los Angeles* (Grand Rapids: Christian Classics Ethereal Library), 102, accessed January 25, 2016, http://www.ccel.org/ccel/bartleman/los.pdf. "One Sunday night the hall was packed out, to the middle of the street. I went to the hall one morning to look up the folks, who had not come home. Several had stayed all night. I found them lost to all but God. They could not get away. A very shekinah glory filled the place. It was awesome, but glorious."

6. Miriam Rockness, "Out-of-print Manuscripts," *Lilias Trotter* (blog), accessed October 4, 2016, https://ililiastrotter.wordpress.com/out-of-print-manu scripts/. The word *attrait* used at the end of this passage was the French word used for "attraction," which Lilias regularly used in her writings. Her song ended with the following quote by Tersteegen:

Hath not each heart a passion and a dream,
Each some companionship for ever sweet,
And each in saddest skies some silver gleam,
And each some passing joy, too fair and fleet,
And each a staff and stay, though frail it prove,
And each a face he fain would ever see?
And what have I? an endless stream of love,
A rapture, and a glory, and a calm
A life that is an everlasting psalm,
All, O Beloved, in Thee.

7. If you need a little help to get started, the Centering Prayer model is a good place to begin. It focuses mostly on the contemplation aspect of the monastic prayer model known as Lectio Divina, emphasizing direct communion and absorption with God Himself. It is the practice of being fully present with God without interruptions or distractions. See "Centering Prayer," Contemplative Outreach, https://www.contemplativeoutreach.org/category/category/centering-prayer, accessed September 8, 2016. See also Thomas Keating, *Open Mind, Open Heart, 20th Anniversary Edition* (London: Bloomsbury, 2006), 11, where he writes that "contemplative prayer is a process within contemplative life. The former is an experience or series of experiences leading to the abiding state of union with God. The term *contemplative life* is the abiding state of divine union itself, in which one is habitually and continuously moved both in prayer and action by the Spirit. Centering prayer is an entrance into the process that leads to divine union. The root of prayer is interior silence."

Chapter 7: Full Attention

1. Caroline Leaf, *Switch on Your Brain: The Key to Peak Happiness, Thinking, and Health* (Grand Rapids, Mich.: Baker, 2013), 94–97.
2. Ibid.

Chapter 8: Forward Momentum

1. See also Jennifer A. Miskov, *Silver to Gold: A Journey of Young Revolutionaries* (Birmingham, U.K.: Silver to Gold, 2009), to read the story of Joshua and Caleb entering the Promised Land repackaged in the form of an allegory.
2. Daniel M. Phillips, *Evan Roberts: The Great Welsh Revivalist and His Work*, 2nd ed. (London: Marshall Brothers, 1906), 215 (available at www.welshrevival .org), from a letter dated November 5, 1904. Since Roberts said this at many meetings, various other versions of this include the following: "You desire an outpouring of the Holy Spirit in your district? Well, four conditions must be observed. They are essential—mark the word, *essential*. (1) Is there any sin in your past that you have not confessed to God? On your knees at once! Your past must be put away

and cleansed. (2) Is there anything in your life that is doubtful—anything you can not decide whether it is good or evil? Away with it! There must not be a trace of a cloud between you and God. Have you forgiven *everybody*—EVERYBODY? If not, don't expect forgiveness for your own sins: you won't get it. (3) Do what the Spirit prompts. Obedience—prompt, implicit, unquestioning obedience to the Spirit of God. (4) A public confession of Christ as your Savior. There is a vast difference between profession and confession. You praise the Father, praise the Son; why don't you praise the Holy Spirit? You speak of Him as 'something!' The Spirit has been smothered in hundreds of churches. Quench not the Spirit. When the fire burns, it purifies, and when purified you are useful for the work of God." S. B. Shaw, "God Hath Visited His People" (from a report in *Bright Woods*), in *The Great Revival in Wales* (Chicago: S. B. Shaw Publisher, 1905), 67–68.

Chapter 11: Resilience

1. Theodore Roosevelt, "Citizenship in a Republic" (speech, La Sorbonne, Paris, France, April 23, 1910), http://www.theodore-roosevelt.com/trsorbonne speech.html.

Chapter 12: Seek First the Kingdom

1. Mel Tari with Cliff Dudley, *Like a Mighty Wind* (Carol Stream, Ill.: Creation House, 1971), 43–46.

2. "Walk on water miracle—Mel Tari," uploaded December 26, 2007, by SacrificeOfPraise, https://youtu.be/93TKE8_4QC0.

3. I had previously published a book entitled *Silver to Gold: A Journey of Young Revolutionaries* (Birmingham, U.K.: Silver to Gold, 2009), which was one of the reasons I felt such heavy conviction in this moment.

4. Read the testimony Jessika Tate wrote about her healing at Jessika Tate, "Healed from PTSD through Dance at Destiny House," *Silver to Gold* (blog), May 18, 2016, http://www.silvertogold.com/blog/jessikatate. You can also watch a video that Bethel.TV produced about this testimony at Jessika Tate, testimony, *Bethel.TV Testimonies*, March 28, 2016, https://www.facebook.com/ibetheltv /videos/10155056516900930/.

Chapter 14: Hunger

1. Carrie Judd Montgomery, "The Life on Wings: The Possibilities of Pentecost," *Triumphs of Faith* 32, no. 8 (August 1912): 169–177. The article was adapted from an address delivered at the Stone Church in Chicago in 1910 and revised by Carrie before she published it. You can read this article in Jennifer A. Miskov, *Life on Wings: The Forgotten Life and Theology of Carrie Judd Montgomery (1858–1946)* (Cleveland, Tenn.: CPT Press, 2012), 310–316.

2. W. Hacking, *Smith Wigglesworth—Remembered* (Tulsa: Harrison House Publishers, 1981), 29–30.

3. See Jennifer A. Miskov, "Feasting on God: The Lost Art of Fasting," *Silver to Gold* (blog), August 24, 2014, http://www.silvertogold.com/blog/2014/08 /22/2014822feasting-on-god-the-lost-art-of-fasting-part-1.

Chapter 16: Courage

1. In Old French in the 1300s the word developed into *corage*, which in addition to "heart" also meant "innermost feelings." In Middle English the word *courage* was used for "what's in one's minds and thoughts." Douglas Harper, *Online Etymology Dictionary*, s.v. "courage," http://www.dictionary.com/browse/courage, accessed January 19, 2017. Some present-day synonyms for this word include *bravery, inner strength, conviction, confidence* and *valor.* To "encourage" means to "hearten" others or to strengthen or add courage to their hearts.

2. Online Parallel Bible Project, "3954. parrésia," Bible Hub, accessed April 12, 2017, http://biblehub.com/greek/3954.htm.

3. See Jennifer A. Miskov, "Love So Extravagantly It Burns Through Offense," *Elijah List*, April 2, 2016, http://www.elijahlist.com/words/display_word.html?ID=15897, or at *Silver to Gold* (blog), March 24, 2016, http://www.silvertogold.com/blog/2016/03/24/extravagantlove.

4. Online Parallel Bible Project, "553. amets," Bible Hub, accessed April 12, 2017, http://biblehub.com/hebrew/553.htm.

5. Helen H. Lemmel, "Turn Your Eyes upon Jesus," 1922, public domain.

Jennifer A. Miskov, Ph.D., loves to lead people into life-changing encounters with Jesus through her writing, teaching and ministry. She is the founding director of Destiny House, a community of worshipers who launch people into their destinies from a place of intimacy with God and connection with family. Established in 2012, Destiny House carries a vision for worship to be stewarded in the context of family for one hundred years and for five thousand worshiping communities to be birthed around the world.

In 2011 Jen received her Ph.D. in global Pentecostal and charismatic studies from the University of Birmingham, U.K. She currently teaches revival history classes at Bethel School of Supernatural Ministry and speaks and ministers around the world. She is the author of *Ignite Azusa: Positioning for a New Jesus Revolution* and also supported Bill Johnson in writing *Defining Moments*. Jen loves to inspire first-time authors to live from their hearts and write their first books through her *Writing in the Glory* book and workshop. She has also written *Life on Wings: The Forgotten Life and Theology of Carrie Judd Montgomery*, *Spirit Flood: Rebirth of Spirit Baptism for the 21st Century*, *Silver to Gold: A Journey of Young Revolutionaries* and more. You can learn more about Jen and Destiny House at www.silvertogold.com.